PRAISE FOR *AI OPTIMISM*

"*AI Optimism* invites educators to see generative AI not as a shortcut but as a springboard for creativity, access, and student voice. Through powerful classroom stories and practical, hands-on strategies, Keene shows what's possible when we move from fear to curiosity and from consumption to collaboration. This book is a call to reimagine what learning can look like in an AI-powered world."

—**Dr. Sabba Quidwai,** CEO, Designing Schools

"Rather than approaching AI with fear or hype, *AI Optimism* offers a grounded road map for educators. It explores how AI can amplify empathy, creativity, and culturally responsive teaching. Framed by the SAMR model, the book encourages thoughtful experimentation and collective learning to ensure AI tools enhance, not erase, the human aspects of education. As someone committed to equity and innovation, I found its message both timely and deeply affirming."

—**Dr. Sonal Patel,** program director, digital learning and computer science education, San Bernardino County Superintendent of Schools

"*AI Optimism* grounds generative AI integration in pedagogical frameworks like SAMR, moving past simple substitution toward genuine transformation. It positions AI not as a threat but as a partner in addressing long-standing educational challenges while emphasizing responsible use, digital citizenship, and ethical applications that shape future-ready learners."

—**Sophia Mendoza,** director, instructional technology initiative, Los Angeles Unified School District; ISTE+ASCD board member

"*AI Optimism* offers a thoughtful and grounded approach to integrating AI in education. By aligning AI use with the SAMR model, it invites educators to move beyond basic applications toward authentic, collaborative innovation. This book recognizes both the promise and the complexity of AI, making space for nuanced conversations around equity, creativity, and responsible use in the classroom."

—**Sharo Dickerson,** director of digital and learning resources, El Paso ISD

"*AI Optimism* is an essential resource that reimagines the classroom as a space for student creativity, agency, and transformation. It highlights how AI can empower learners and educators to break past outdated constraints and uncertainties. The book is a must-read for leaders ready to shift from fear to opportunity and champion ethical, student-centered innovation."

—**Laurie Kirkland,** head of digital learning, AVID Center

"Keene brilliantly weaves the SAMR framework with real classroom insight to show how AI can transform learning in ways that matter for truly all students. This book pushes us to move beyond fear and embrace the future our students are already living in—one where redefinition isn't optional, it's necessary."

—**Dr. Natasha Rachell,** director of instructional technology, Atlanta Public Schools

"Keene presents a hopeful and practical framework for integrating artificial intelligence in education through a thoughtful and realistic lens. Rather than viewing AI as a replacement for educators, she frames it as a partner in transforming instructional practice. By connecting AI tools to SAMR's progression, Becky encourages educators to move beyond surface-level uses of technology and instead focus on enhancing student agency, deepening learning, and designing future-ready classrooms."

—**Stevie Frank,** technology integration specialist, Zionsville Community Schools

"*AI Optimism* invites educators to confront and then reimagine the purpose of school in an era shaped by generative AI. Rather than defaulting to tools that automate outdated and ineffective practices, Keene calls for a human-centered transformation of the learning experience. While the SAMR model offers a useful entry point for integrating AI into classroom practice, the book pushes beyond it—encouraging educators to challenge traditional assumptions, prioritize student agency, and create entirely new possibilities for learning. Through concrete examples and an approachable voice, Keene offers not just a framework, but a provocation: What kind of learning do we really want to see, and what role should AI play in helping us build it?"

—**Dr. LeeAnn Lindsey,** director, edtech and innovation, Arizona Institute for Education and the Economy, Northern Arizona University

"Keene reaches all educators with this new book—from the most resistant to change to the most tech-savvy evangelist. I love that Keene uses the SAMR ideology. It makes complete sense, and it's different than what I've seen from other books on AI. I would recommend this book to every educator, whether they use AI daily or have barely dipped a toe in. Embracing AI usage, with the help of a tool like Keene's book, could change a student's whole life perspective!"

—**Melody McAllister,** executive director, Alaska Society for Technology in Education (ASTE)

"*AI Optimism* energizes educators ready to embrace the possibilities of generative AI. Rather than just automating old tasks, Becky shows how AI can spark creativity, personalize learning, and open entirely new experiences for students and teachers alike. With warmth and vision, she offers a pathway for exploring AI in classrooms that's grounded in pedagogy, filled with real examples, and always centered on human connection."

—**Dyane Smokorowski,** coordinator of digital literacy, Wichita Public Schools; 2013 Kansas Teacher of the Year

"*AI Optimism* is the book I've been waiting for. As an instructional technology coach and classroom teacher, I've long used SAMR to guide our staff, and Becky Keene seamlessly bridges that familiar framework with the emerging world of AI. The book is filled with realistic examples that show how AI can transform—not just streamline—education. It's an essential read for coaches looking to lead AI integration in their districts with purpose and clarity."

—**Callie Salaymeh,** PhD, instructional technology coach, Lyons Township High School District 204

"*AI Optimism* is a rare blend of clarity, inspiration, and practical vision. Becky Keene goes beyond tools—she gives us the language and structure to lead thoughtful, scalable innovations. It's an essential resource for educators and instructional leaders seeking to support and lift their learning communities with intention and imagination."

—**Starian Porchia,** MA, MEd, community builder, learning designer, and consultant

"As a high school CTE teacher, *AI Optimism* resonates deeply with my mission to prepare students for the future. This book is a timely and inspiring guide that challenges us to move beyond using AI as a shortcut and instead see it as a collaborative partner for creativity and transformation."

—**Tisha Richmond,** culinary arts / CTE teacher, Medford School District

"*AI Optimism* is a foundational guide for educators navigating the role of artificial intelligence. Keene challenges educators to lead with integrity, prioritize ethical use, and embrace a vision where technology enhances—not replaces—human-centered learning. This is a must-read for teachers, coaches, and education leaders ready to move from curiosity to confident, meaningful AI implementation."

—**Jennifer Womble,** chair, FETC and District Administration

"*AI Optimism* offers a practical framework for integrating generative AI into education. This book guides educators through a progression of AI use from efficiency to true transformation. Keene emphasizes thoughtful design, responsible use, and pedagogical integrity while helping educators avoid common pitfalls like tool-first thinking."

—**Dr. Karina Quilantan-Garza,** library media specialist; 2022 Librarian of the Year, Texas Library Association

"*AI Optimism* is a practical, hopeful guide. It helps educators move from automation to imagination, positioning AI as a catalyst for creativity, agency, and authentic learning for both students and staff."

—**Melissa Benner,** innovation and technology coordinator, Peninsula School District

"*AI Optimism* guides educators to navigate the rapidly evolving world of generative artificial intelligence. Keene provides not just tools, but a clear pedagogical framework that, along with SAMR, helps educators think critically about how AI can truly enhance learning. The book's emphasis on meaningful integration and learner agency makes it a valuable resource for both new and experienced practitioners."

—**Alana Winnick,** educational technology director, Pocantico Hills CSD; author, *The Generative Age*; Withrow Chief Technology Officer of the Year, CoSN 2025

"Becky Keene offers a refreshing and forward-thinking perspective on the use of artificial intelligence in education. Rather than promoting fear or resistance, this book encourages educators to view AI as a tool to enhance their professional practice. With a focus on innovation, equity, and student-centered design. *AI Optimism* emphasizes the importance of human agency, ethical considerations, and digital literacy as foundational elements of future-ready instruction."

—**Niyoka D. McCoy, EdD,** chief learning officer, Stride, Inc.

AI OPTIMISM

AI OPTIMISM

A Guide to Redefining
Artificial Intelligence
in Education

BECKY KEENE

Foreword by Ruben R. Puentedura, PhD

AI OPTIMISM
© 2025 Becky Keene

All rights reserved. No part of this publication may be reproduced in any form or by any electronic or mechanical means, including information storage and retrieval systems, without permission in writing by the publisher, except by a reviewer who may quote brief passages in a review. For information regarding permission, contact the publisher at books@daveburgessconsulting.com.

> This book is available at special discounts when purchased in quantity for educational purposes or for use as premiums, promotions, or fundraisers. For inquiries and details, contact the publisher at books@daveburgessconsulting.com.

Published by Dave Burgess Consulting, Inc.
Vancouver, WA
DaveBurgessConsulting.com

Library of Congress Control Number: 2025940501
Paperback ISBN: 978-1-956306-97-2
Ebook ISBN: 978-1-956306-98-9

Cover and interior design by Liz Schreiter
Edited and produced by Reading List Editorial
ReadingListEditorial.com

For the dreamer

CONTENTS

Foreword by Ruben R. Puentedura, PhD 1
Introduction: Who and What Is This Book For? 5

Part I: Foundation and Framework

1: The Problem with AI in Education 10
   Spotting the Symptoms 10
      Barrier #1: Tool-First Thinking 11
      Barrier #2: Overwhelming Options 11
      Barrier #3: Floating Around Framework-Free 12
   Cost and Consequences 12
   Fixing the Flaws 13
   The Book's Structure 14
   How to Use This Book 15
      Getting Started 15

2: SAMR: The Solution 17
   The SAMR Framework 18
      SAMR Through Social Media 18
      SAMR Beyond Digital Tools 19
      Distinguishing Between SAMR Levels 21
   SAMR and Artificial Intelligence 22
   Addressing a Common Concern About SAMR 22

3: Previously Unimaginable: What AI + SAMR Makes Possible .. 24
   Transforming Assessment 26
   Removing Barriers to Creation 27
   Personalizing Learning at Scale 28
   AI Optimism: A New Educational Paradigm 29

4: First Steps 32
   The Journey Ahead 32
   Praxis 34
   Privacy 39
   Prompting 43

Part II: The SAMR Journey Through Educational Tasks

5: Design **50**
- Substitution 52
  - Project Plans 52
  - Working with Standards 53
- Augmentation 56
  - Mind Mapping 56
- Modification 57
  - Course Catalog 57
  - Culturally Responsive and Universally Designed Content 60
  - Immersive Spaces 62
  - Unit Planning 64
  - Infographics 65
- Conclusion 67

6: Create **69**
- Substitution 71
  - Create Questions for Quizzes or Discussions 71
  - Create Student Surveys 75
  - Generate Discussion Responses 76
  - Draft Communications 79
  - Written Work 81
- Augmentation 85
  - Content Generation 85
- Modification 89
  - Video Engagement 89
  - Exemplars 91
- Conclusion 98

7: Support **100**
- Substitution 102
  - AI-Powered Literacy Support 102
  - Frequently Asked Questions 103
  - Information Searches (Research) 104
  - Math Solution Checker 107
- Augmentation 110
  - Learner Chatbots 110
  - Personalized Learning Platforms 112
  - Personalized PD Plans and Virtual Coaching 113
- Modification 116
  - College/Career Guidance 116
  - Competency-Based Skill Building 119
  - Debate 120

    Fluency Practice 122
    Identify Challenges 123
    Mental Health Support 129
    Self-Coaching 130
    Talk to a Character 132
    Thought Partner 135
  Conclusion 136

8: Analyze 139
  Substitution 141
    Data Analysis 141
    Summaries of Presentations or Spreadsheets 142
  Augmentation 143
    Attendance Reporting 143
    Meeting Summaries 145
    Predictive Analytics 146
    Research Assistance 147
  Conclusion 149

9: Evaluate 152
  Substitution 154
    Creating Assessment Supports 154
    Observing, Evaluating, and Modeling 158
  Augmentation 159
    Grading and Assessment 159
    Speaking Skills 160
    Performance Analysis 162
    Progress Monitoring 165
  Conclusion 167

10: Manage 170
  Substitution 172
    Meeting Scheduling 172
  Augmentation 173
    Discussion Moderation 173
    Note-Taking 174
    Personalized Study Plans 175
    Translation 178
  Modification 180
    Computer Vision 180
    Mind Mapping 182
    Policy Development 186
    Scheduling 192
  Conclusion 195

Part III: Redefinition and Beyond

11: Redefinition 198
    Content Creation and Writing 201
    Virtual Companions 201
    AI-Generated Art Exhibitions 202
    AI-Powered Storytelling 202
    Personalized Music Composition 202
    Elementary Learners: Virtual Field Trips with Interactive Elements 204
    Middle School Learners: Collaborative Global Projects 204
    Secondary School Leaners: Prototype Designing and Building 204
    Prompt Vocabulary 206
    Real-World Data Sets 208
    Assessment Swap 210
    Promptathons and Prompt Libraries 211
    Microcredentials 212
    Physical Space Construction 215
    Curiosity Coaching 216
    Team Coaching 217
    Career Exploration 217
    Video Avatars 219
    Video Creation 220
    Game Creation 224
    Song Creation 226
    Illustrations 228
    Scavenger Hunts and Escape Rooms 229
    Simulations and Interactives 232
    Audio Overview 234
    Conclusion 235

12: Closing 237

Appendix 241
    Teacher Self-Assessment 242
    Administrator Self-Assessment 246

Acknowledgments 251
About Becky Keene 252
More from Dave Burgess Consulting, Inc. 254

FOREWORD
BY RUBEN R. PUENTEDURA, PHD

THE UNVEILING OF CHATGPT IN November 2022 opened up a new world of possibilities for uses of AI in education. AI had already been in use in multiple forms for many years, of course, over a wide range of learning domains, applications, and approaches. But the particularly powerful and plastic nature of ChatGPT, as well as its simple conversational interface, was taken by many to herald a new world of "transparent" education tools that would run in the background of the learning process without requiring much change. The power was—and is—very real, but that transparency is not. Generative AI (GenAI) is no more or less transparent than any other learning technology that has preceded it, from reeds scribbling cuneiform on wet clay tablets to video streams bringing students into shared online spaces. And like any technology, GenAI's impact upon learners will depend on how their use of it relates to what they were doing before it came on the scene. This is where Becky Keene's new book, which you're now reading, plays a crucial role.

As I write these words, large language models (LLMs) such as the one underlying ChatGPT have expanded from short and simple textual prompt processing to "reasoning." They are now capable of more complex and lengthy chain-of-thought processes, and they can integrate provided documents to augment their knowledge store. LLMs are also rapidly evolving from text-only incarnations to omnimodal versions that can handle a range of inputs and outputs as code, images, audio, video, and more. However, the key challenges for educators remain the same as with other prior technologies. Keene identifies many of them—tool-first thinking, an overwhelming range of options, the lack of a guiding framework, and missed opportunities resulting from all three—and addresses them expertly, using (much to my delight) the SAMR model.

On that last challenge—missed opportunities—let me take a moment to expand upon Keene's thoughts. She crucially identifies lost opportunities for enrichment of students' current educational experiences and their readiness for the future (including jobs). In this context, I would like to stress a point that she already makes: The learner's *agency*, not just over their immediate learning process (as mediated or enhanced by AI) but also over their future lives, is critical. It's a given that the AI tool set will form part of their future, including work; that they will retain control over how to use these tools is not. Early, thoughtful, and transformative use of AI is essential to this latter aspect, as Keene explains. Using the AI tool set for learning can scaffold deeper and richer use in daily life, and it can also lead to an understanding of AI's power in shaping jobs that expand and enrich the individual's experience. This goes far beyond just having AI take over tasks here and there.

As one example, since the economic crisis of 2008, recent college graduates have enjoyed a progressively smaller (and lately negative) advantage where unemployment rates are concerned. There are multiple reasons for this phenomenon, but introduction of AI into a workplace where individuals understand and control it poorly is likely to aggravate it. By contrast, a learner who understands and uses AI at a deep level, not just to replace boring or routine tasks but to take their thinking in new directions, can leverage the knowledge and skills gained throughout their education career to overcome employment challenges.

It is often easier to diagnose problems than to show how to solve them. Fortunately, to illustrate solutions, Keene develops both a framework and exemplars to create what she terms a lens of *AI optimism*, a description that I like very much. The six educational processes that ground her framework—design, create, support, analyze, evaluate, and manage—provide a powerful and systematic scaffold for the introduction of AI in education, guided by SAMR-based thinking. I'd strongly encourage you, the reader, to engage with each of these processes in an active frame of mind: Think of a learning challenge you'd dearly love students to undertake, one that could radically reshape their thinking and would not vanish into the depths of "Oh, yeah, I think we talked about that in fifth grade . . . " Then, consider how you might go through each one of these processes (with your SAMR glasses on) to make the challenge come alive. Who knows, you might even engage the assistance of a GenAI engine (or two) to help you out.

Let me cite one example from my own practice to illustrate the power of this process. We have already exceeded the 1.5 degrees Celsius warming threshold in 2024, and it is unlikely that this will remain only an unusual fluctuation in the years to come. This will have multiple negative impacts upon the lives of the children who are in our classrooms today—but I refuse to infuse their learning with nothing more than a sense of hopeless pessimism. Instead, I work with teachers to see how GenAI can be used to transform how students think about their own lives and agency in this emerging world. We've always asked students to draw pictures of themselves and their communities in the future—but now learners can use GenAI to help them do the following:

- Create dozens of alternative approaches to living in the future climate, ranging from minor changes in their current homes to dramatic transformations such as migrating.
- Leverage these variations to ask "what if" questions that suggest paths worth exploring or discarding.
- Recognize, analyze, and integrate the illustrations created by multiple students, helping identify complementary and contradictory elements and mediate a new shared vision.
- Synthesize video that illustrates navigating these worlds, illuminating challenges not realized or understood in static form, leading to more questions and refinements.

- Generate code that simulates key aspects of the projected communities, helping ground these futures by exploring how to make parts of them into reality.

Everything I have just described can be done today, with low-cost and accessible GenAI tools that are available to any learner with a laptop, tablet, or smartphone. The details of implementing AI in the classroom, using Keene's framework, will be left as an exercise for the reader . . .

In closing, I can only say it has been a delight to read this book, and I hope others will find Becky Keene's work as thoughtful and useful—indeed, as redefining—as I have. And you might want to keep a couple of GenAI tools at hand while you peruse it—it's the kind of book that calls for immediate and direct action and exploration.

Ruben R. Puentedura, PhD
May 2025

INTRODUCTION

WHO AND WHAT IS THIS BOOK FOR?

You have arrived at the prestigious Arcane Academy of Enchanted Arts, where only the most promising young wizards and witches are accepted. The grand castle-like academy stands atop a misty hill, its towering spires crackling with latent magic. The halls hum with the whispers of centuries-old spells, and ancient portraits watch your every move with knowing eyes.

As you settle into your dormitory on the first night, a parchment materializes on your desk, inscribed with shimmering ink:

Knowledge is hidden in the shadows. Seek the glyph of the First Mage before the third moon wanes.

A thrill courses through you. Could this be a test? A secret society? Or something more dangerous? The note offers no answers, only the beginning of a journey.

Do you (a) follow the note's clue or (b) seek help from a classmate?

Turn the page when you're ready to continue.

What did you choose? At the very least, you turned the page—and that tells me you might be hooked already!

This AI-generated story is a response I got to a prompt that I saw circulating online and decided to test out. It was just days after ChatGPT became publicly available, and I sat down with my kids at home to create personalized stories where we controlled the narrative. We were captivated—not by a video game or social media, but by reading and making predictions, comparing story paths, and engaging deeply with text. My kids were experiencing literature in a way that was interactive, personalized, and genuinely exciting.

In that moment, I glimpsed the transformational potential of generative AI in education. Not just as a fancy tool to grade tests or generate worksheets, though it can certainly do those things—but as a vehicle for reimagining what learning could look like.

What would you say if someone suggested that the most sophisticated, resource-intensive technology in the world could make your students more engaged and curious learners? What if AI could help your students express themselves in ways they never thought possible? What if it allowed them to create things that weren't previously possible? If you're like me, you'd say yes immediately! But the reality of how AI is being introduced to education doesn't always match this vision. The potential is there, but the implementation often falls short.

When generative AI became all anyone could talk about at education conferences, I watched sparkly new apps pop up claiming they could save teachers time by generating worksheets and quizzes and lesson plans. I got concerned. I remembered seeing the same themes surface twenty years ago with student devices and increased internet access. Similar worries, similar adoption issues, similar promises. I could see the value of just getting started with generative AI by outsourcing everyday tasks, but I also (more importantly) could see amazing possibilities to transform education. I started talking, posting, speaking, sharing, and writing about shifting our focus from low-level to high-level impact. I was honored to get great feedback on how my approach was helping people see the immediate application and future possibilities of generative AI in meaningful, positive ways.

For the past two and a half years, I've been immersed in the world of AI and education, helping develop training materials for Microsoft's Copilot and other tools, visiting classrooms, teaching students, and most importantly, listening to educators' hopes and concerns. I've witnessed skeptical teachers shift from *never* to *not yet* and then *maybe now* as they discovered AI's potential—not as a replacement for teaching but as a powerful tool for enhancing learning. Best of all, I've seen students light up when AI helped them overcome barriers to expression and creation.

If you're wondering how to get started with generative AI in your daily life, this book is for you. If you're already using GenAI regularly, this book is also for you. If you're a teacher, a learning designer, an instructional coach, a head of a school, a professor, or an IT admin, this book is especially for you. I've organized it in a way that I hope allows you to dig into ideas and possibilities that best meet your needs. I also hope this book can build awareness of new opportunities to integrate AI while advocating for appropriate, targeted use.

Throughout my career, I've watched education adopt technology without a clear framework for integration. We introduce new tools without modifying the tasks they support. The result? Technology becomes a more expensive, more complicated way to do the same old things.

That's why this book revolves around the SAMR model. It's a framework that helps us move beyond merely substituting traditional methods with digital tools and toward using technology to create learning experiences that were previously impossible. I believe it's the perfect lens through which to approach AI in education.

You can read one section at a time, or even just one activity at a time. Or you can read the whole thing, choose some ideas to try at each level, and discuss with your colleagues. My goal is to provide support in choosing the right tool for the right purpose and to encourage everyone to consider ways to use generative AI that truly transform education.

The question isn't whether AI will change education, because it already is. The question is whether we'll use it merely to automate the status quo or to reimagine what's possible. This book is your invitation to be on the front line of that transformation.

PART I
FOUNDATION AND FRAMEWORK

THE PROBLEM WITH AI IN EDUCATION

"**LOOKING FOR WAYS TO USE** pencils with my students. Does anyone know a good place to start?"

Can you imagine seeing a post like that on social media?

Of course not. Yet every day, I see educators posting similar questions about AI. These are educators who are eager to embrace new technology but don't know where to begin. They're overwhelmed, uncertain, and often intimidated by the very tools that could benefit their teaching. And I don't blame them! This scenario is the central problem this book aims to address. In our rush to adopt AI in education, we're often using sophisticated technology for mundane tasks or, worse, using it in ways that reinforce outdated teaching methods rather than transform them.

SPOTTING THE SYMPTOMS

Social media is full of primary teachers, secondary teachers, building administrators, school leaders, system coordinators, and university faculty who are looking for ways to save time, be more creative, prepare students for a future world steeped in AI, and keep kids safe. If you're reading this, I'm guessing you can identify with some or all of this list. (I'm active on social media, and my TikTalkWalks are designed to give helpful, daily, bite-sized tips and thoughts around implementing AI. There are so many ways to learn and get help!)

I recently observed an app company that was proud to show off how educators were using generative AI. The company was promoting a new feature that would allow educators to paste the URL of an engaging YouTube video into the tool and have it generate a presentation summarizing the video's content. "Look how much time this saves!" the company shared on its social channels.

I couldn't help but be disappointed. Think with me about what was happening there: taking dynamic, interactive content that students could engage with at their own pace—pausing, rewinding, following their curiosity—and converting it into static slides for a teacher-centered lecture. Technology was being used, certainly, but in a way that moved backward pedagogically.

The struggle with adopting AI has several dimensions. Let's explore three barriers preventing effective implementation.

Barrier #1: Tool-First Thinking

Many educators approach AI forums and communities with questions like "Looking for ways to use AI with my students." These well-intentioned questions start from the wrong place. It's focused on a tool rather than the learning objectives. Without providing context about what they're teaching, their students' ages, or their educational goals, teachers can't get meaningful guidance. When we lead with technology instead of pedagogy, we're already on shaky ground.

Barrier #2: Overwhelming Options

When an educator asks for help with AI, they'll usually get a lot of tool-centric responses. While recommendations are helpful, getting a long list of apps that have worked for other people can be overwhelming. Many start free and have a paid option, most claim to save teachers time, some include student use, and all should be vetted for data privacy compliance. I saw a post the other day in which the author finally commented, "How are these tools different? How do I choose where to start?"

This overwhelm is compounded by the fact that educators are already inundated with digital platforms their districts have purchased. Clunky learning management systems, assessment tools with confusing interfaces, and student information systems all come to mind. No wonder many of us approach yet another technology with skepticism or dread.

Unlike those platforms, however, generative AI represents a fundamental shift in how we interact with technology. Instead of navigating complex menus and learning proprietary systems, you can simply talk to AI in natural language. The barrier to entry is considerably lower—but that doesn't mean educators (or students!) automatically know how to use it effectively.

Barrier #3: Floating Around Framework-Free

Even when they've identified a good tool and a clear purpose, many educators might default to using powerful technology for mundane tasks. I see sophisticated AI being used to generate multiple-choice quizzes or vocabulary lists. These are tasks that don't leverage AI's unique capabilities or transform the learning experience at all. Teachers, schools, and systems sometimes adopt these solutions without a vision for how technology could fundamentally enhance or redefine education. Without such a framework, we risk expensive, time-consuming implementation that delivers minimal educational value.

COST AND CONSEQUENCES

The consequences of a poor approach to AI are significant—when it is misused or used ineffectively, we see backlash and restrictions. I've seen students lose access to their laptop as punishment for misbehavior on the playground; this restricts academic opportunity over an unrelated infraction. But I now see students who misuse ChatGPT lose access to all AI tools, including those that might provide crucial support for their learning needs.

Perhaps the most dramatic missed opportunity, though, is failing to prepare students for their futures. By focusing on having AI perform tasks like summarizing content or creating presentations—tasks machines will increasingly do in the workplace—we miss the chance to develop the uniquely human skills our students will need, like critical thinking, creativity, ethical reasoning, and discernment.

FIXING THE FLAWS

Sometimes I'm quick to love new technology, usually because it fits a very specific need I've seen for a while. However, digital tools should be carefully selected so they improve teaching and learning, not get in the way. For years, I've been quoting what Robert Baker once said to me: "It's not about the device—until you have the wrong one." It's true, but even the best tools can fail if they're not utilized correctly—we need a model and a framework that guides users to solutions, creative approaches to age-old problems, and a strong vision for how to improve educational outcomes. That's exactly what I hope to provide.

> EVEN THE BEST TOOLS CAN FAIL IF THEY'RE NOT UTILIZED CORRECTLY.

> Don't wait until you feel completely ready to begin your AI journey. Like learning to swim, some things can only be learned by doing. Take that first step, knowing that each small success builds confidence for the next.

THE BOOK'S STRUCTURE

This book is designed to be both a pathway and a resource. Consider it a journey you can follow from start to finish and a guide you can consult whenever you need inspiration or direction. Let me explain how it's organized to help you get the most from it.

PART I—FOUNDATION AND FRAMEWORK: The first few chapters lay the groundwork for understanding how AI and the SAMR model work together to change education. We begin by exploring the problem with how AI is currently being introduced in education, then dive into the SAMR framework as a solution. After examining what becomes possible when we combine AI with this framework, we'll cover essential first steps, including using effective prompting techniques, addressing plagiarism concerns, and navigating privacy considerations. This foundation will prepare you for the more practical applications that follow.

PART II—THE SAMR JOURNEY THROUGH EDUCATIONAL TASKS: The heart of this book is organized around the fundamental tasks of education: design, create, support, analyze, evaluate, and manage. This structure follows the natural flow of teaching and learning, whether you're acting as a teacher, leader, or learner. We *design* learning experiences and systems; *create* content, materials, resources, and work products; *support* the learning process; *analyze* data and responses; *evaluate* outcomes and effectiveness; and throughout, *manage* the many moving parts of education.

Within each of these task-based chapters, you'll find a progressive journey through the first three levels of the SAMR model. I've provided tasks that are specific to each role and labeled substitution, augmentation, or modification.

PART III—REDEFINITION AND BEYOND: The final section focuses exclusively on the redefinition level of SAMR. This is where applications of AI make entirely new tasks possible. This warrants its own section because redefinition often blurs the traditional lines between educational roles. When learning is truly changed, students become designers, creators, and analysts alongside their teachers. This chapter showcases the revolutionary potential of AI when we move beyond conventional educational boundaries.

HOW TO USE THIS BOOK

There's no single right way to use this resource. You might:

- Read it cover to cover with sticky notes and highlighters, marking ideas to try later
- Use it as a guidebook, flipping to relevant sections when you need guidance on a specific task
- Treat it like a recipe book, consulting it during lesson planning or when you're looking for something new to try
- Reference it as a professional development tool for yourself or your colleagues

Whichever approach you choose, I recommend keeping this book accessible. It could be on your desk, beside your computer, or wherever you plan lessons. It's designed to be a resource you'll return to repeatedly as your AI journey evolves.

Getting Started

As you explore the possibilities in these pages, remember two key principles:

1. **Safety first:** Ensure any tools you use comply with your school's guidelines and data privacy practices. I've included considerations throughout to help you navigate these issues, but ultimately you are responsible for the tools you use.
2. **Start small:** Incremental innovation sticks better than dramatic overhauls. Choose one idea to implement rather than try to alter everything at once. This approach builds confidence and competence while allowing you to evaluate what works best for your context.

Whether you're a classroom teacher looking to enhance student engagement, a learning designer seeking efficient workflows, an administrator exploring school-wide implementation, or an IT professional supporting educational technology, this book offers practical pathways to get all you want from AI's potential through the proven SAMR framework.

SAMR: THE SOLUTION

SAMR IS A FRAMEWORK DEVELOPED by Dr. Ruben Puentedura to help educators integrate technology into teaching and learning effectively. When I learned about it while working as an instructional coach, it immediately resonated with me. At the time, my school district in Kent, Washington, had just finished rolling out laptops to every middle schooler and educator, and we were focused on helping teachers understand how to use these devices impactfully.

I remember walking into a classroom where a talented English teacher was having students type their essays on their new laptops instead of writing them by hand. She was proud of this digital transition, and so was I. Then I used my coaching strategies to ask, "How do you think this is changing the learning experience for your students?"

Her pause was telling. She realized the task was merely substituted, not transformed. The next week, I returned to find her students using collaborative documents to peer review each others' work in real time, adding comments and suggestions that sparked lively discussions across the room. The energy was palpable. By the end of the semester, her students were publishing multimedia literary analyses incorporating audio interviews, video dramatizations, and interactive timelines—work that would have been inconceivable without digital tools and a teacher willing to overhaul her practice.

> If you already understand SAMR thoroughly, you might choose to skim this section or jump ahead. But you might still discover something new!

Witnessing this journey through the SAMR model confirmed for me the framework's power not just as a theoretical concept but as a practical road map for meaningful technology integration. Teachers didn't need to transform everything overnight; they could evolve their practice deliberately, step by step.

THE SAMR FRAMEWORK

SAMR stands for substitution, augmentation, modification, and redefinition, providing a ladder for educators to progress through four levels of technology integration:

1. **Substitution:** Technology acts as a direct substitute for traditional methods, with no functional change.
2. **Augmentation:** Technology substitutes traditional methods with some functional improvements.
3. **Modification:** Technology allows for significant task redesign.
4. **Redefinition:** Technology enables the creation of new tasks that were previously inconceivable.

Let's explore some real-world examples to illuminate each level.

SAMR Through Social Media

Imagine the SAMR model as the evolution of using a social media platform:

SUBSTITUTION: You sign up for Instagram to direct message friends instead of texting them or to follow a page instead of subscribing to email newsletters. You're keeping in touch with the same people in essentially the same way but with a new tool.

AUGMENTATION: You use hashtags to categorize content, customize notification settings to see less noise, and follow content aligned with your interests. You're using additional features to enhance your experience.

MODIFICATION: You create your own page or group, becoming a content creator rather than just a consumer. You're moderating comments and determining conversation topics, fundamentally changing your role.

REDEFINITION: You leverage the platform to create a viral campaign that sparks global action. You're changing minds and inspiring others to engage with topics in entirely new ways, something inconceivable without this technology.

SAMR Beyond Digital Tools

SAMR's principles extend beyond technology. Consider gardening:

> **SUBSTITUTION:** Start with planting seeds in a pot instead of the ground.
>
> **AUGMENTATION:** Use enhanced tools like watering cans with measurements or soil pH testers that make gardening more efficient.
>
> **MODIFICATION:** Implement advanced techniques like companion planting or hydroponics that significantly change the gardening process and outcomes.
>
> **REDEFINITION:** Create a self-sustaining permaculture garden that maintains its own fertility cycle—something impossible with traditional methods.

While this gardening example likely involves technology at higher levels, notice how the framework illustrates transformative potential regardless of context. Technology is the vehicle, but improved outcomes are the goal.

The power of SAMR, whether applied to education, gardening, or any field, lies in its ability to systematically move us toward more meaningful transformation. On a broader scale, improved outcomes become possible because the framework guides us to think beyond mere adoption of new tools, helping us fundamentally reimagine processes and outcomes.

With AI and education specifically, we see tangible improvements at each step on the ladder. At the substitution level, we might save time with automated grading. At augmentation, we enhance feedback with personalized recommendations. When we reach modification, we can redesign assessments to better reflect real-world challenges. And at redefinition, we create entirely new learning experiences that develop the critical-thinking and creativity skills students will need in an increasingly AI-driven world.

The power of SAMR is that it provides a road map for meaningful progress instead of allowing technology to dictate our direction. Just as the permaculture garden creates sustainable abundance through system redesign rather than just better fertilizer, education through the SAMR lens creates deeper learning through pedagogical innovation rather than digitization of traditional practices.

THE SAMR LENS CREATES DEEPER LEARNING THROUGH PEDAGOGICAL INNOVATION

Distinguishing Between SAMR Levels

Understanding the differences between SAMR levels can sometimes be challenging. Here's a practical guide.

AUGMENTATION VS. MODIFICATION

Augmentation enhances a task with technology, making it more efficient without fundamentally changing its nature.

For example:

- Students research water cycles and write letters to local leaders using a word processor's spell check and comments features.
- Learners create digital flash cards instead of paper ones, adding multimedia elements to aid memory.

Modification significantly redesigns a task in ways that couldn't be accomplished effectively with traditional methods alone.

For example:

- Students collaborate to create multimedia presentations combining research, data, images, and videos, then publish them to a global audience.
- Learners engage in flipped learning where content is delivered at home through interactive videos, preserving class time for hands-on activities and investigations.

When determining whether an activity is augmentation or modification, ask the following:

- Does technology add features that improve the task? (This is augmentation.)
- Does it allow for a redesign that creates new learning opportunities? (This is modification.)

MODIFICATION VS. REDEFINITION

The distinction between these higher levels is more subtle:

Modification alters existing tasks, making them more collaborative, creative, or connected, but the task remains recognizable in its traditional form.

Redefinition creates entirely new tasks that were previously inconceivable, transcending traditional educational boundaries.

For example, a modification project might have students create an interactive digital map of the global water crisis, embedding multimedia resources they've curated.

A redefinition project might have students design a virtual reality experience that simulates the challenges faced by communities with limited clean water access. Then students share this experience globally to inspire action and empathy.

SAMR AND ARTIFICIAL INTELLIGENCE

While SAMR has proved valuable for integrating all forms of technology into education, it's particularly well suited for guiding our approach to artificial intelligence. As we stand at the beginning of an AI revolution in education, SAMR provides the clarity and direction needed to move beyond mere substitution—using AI to generate worksheets or grade multiple-choice tests—toward truly innovative applications.

The progressive nature of SAMR aligns perfectly with how educators can gradually build confidence with AI. Beginning with simple substitution tasks allows for low-risk entry points, while the framework continually challenges us to evolve our practice toward more meaningful implementation.

ADDRESSING A COMMON CONCERN ABOUT SAMR

Some critics argue SAMR is too focused on tools rather than pedagogy. I believe this misses the point—SAMR is deeply pedagogical. It encourages educators to move beyond merely substituting traditional methods with digital tools and consider how technology can fundamentally transform the learning experience.

At the modification stage, teachers design new tasks using digital tools, fundamentally changing the learning activity and requiring deep pedagogical understanding. At the redefinition stage, technology enables previously unimaginable tasks, which can only be realized with strong pedagogical foundations.

Remember that not all lessons, units, or courses need to reach redefinition. There is a time and place for all types of learning activities. Educators should view SAMR as a menu of options to meet the specific needs of their learners and learning outcomes.

In the next chapter, we'll explore the previously unimaginable educational experiences that emerge when we reach the transformation level of SAMR. As we'll discover, AI's unique capabilities make it especially powerful for reaching those higher levels, opening doors to learning experiences that were impossible before.

PREVIOUSLY UNIMAGINABLE

WHAT AI + SAMR MAKES POSSIBLE

IMAGINE A CLASSROOM WHERE A student who struggles with writing due to dyslexia is crafting an eloquent essay, guiding an AI assistant to help structure his thoughts while maintaining his unique voice. Nearby, another student who has never written a line of code is building a fully functional app that tracks local wildlife sightings, using AI to translate her ideas into programming language. Meanwhile, their teacher is reviewing personalized analytics that show not just what students know but their misconceptions when solving math puzzles. The teacher sees learning gaps that would have been missed before.

I saw a glimpse of this potential when visiting a middle school science classroom. Let's call the student Jake. He was a seventh grader who typically avoided writing assignments, but he was using an AI tool to help organize his thoughts for a climate change project. His teacher had noticed he could verbalize complex ideas fluently but would shut down when faced with a blank page.

With the AI assistant, Jake would speak his ideas aloud, then edit and refine the generated text. "It's like having my own personal thinking buddy," he explained to me. "I know what I want to say, but getting started was always the hardest part." His final project showed a depth of understanding that had previously been hidden behind his writing challenges.

What struck me wasn't just the quality of his work but how the technology had revealed capabilities his teachers hadn't fully recognized before. The AI hadn't done the thinking for him. It had simply removed the barrier between his thoughts and their expression. Sometimes the most powerful technology isn't the one that teaches new content but the one that allows students to demonstrate what they already know.

This isn't science fiction. This is education at the redefinition level of SAMR with artificial intelligence. It's happening right now in forward-thinking classrooms around the world.

AI has been supporting humans for years. I won't attempt to write up a history of it here, but if you're interested, just ask your favorite GPT to write a history for you, in your preferred language, with the level of detail you need. This book is focused on today—and the extraordinary tomorrow that's suddenly within our reach.

What makes this moment different from previous technological revolutions in education, however, is the unprecedented combination of power and accessibility. While one-to-one device initiatives took decades to reach widespread adoption (and still haven't reached all students), and reliable internet access remains a challenge in many communities, generative AI became globally accessible almost overnight. Anyone with a mobile device and internet connection, whether they're in a well-funded suburban school or a remote rural classroom, can access the same powerful AI capabilities, largely for free.

This democratization of access creates an opportunity that previous educational technologies simply couldn't match. Let's explore what that transformation looks like when we apply the SAMR model to AI in education.

TRANSFORMING ASSESSMENT

Perhaps no area of education is riper for fundamental shift than assessment. In a world where AI can instantly generate essays, solve complex math problems, and create multimedia presentations, traditional assessments become outdated and irrelevant.

At the redefinition level, we stop asking students to produce work that AI can easily generate. Instead, we challenge them to create things that require uniquely human capabilities: critical evaluation, creative synthesis, ethical judgment, and innovative problem-solving.

Picture a history assessment where, instead of writing a summary of the American Civil War (which AI can do quite well), students analyze AI-generated narratives from different perspectives, identifying biases and questioning assumptions. They then create their own multimedia exhibit that presents the conflict through multiple lenses, demonstrating not just knowledge of facts but deep historical thinking.

Or imagine a science assessment where students use AI to analyze real environmental data from their community, design experiments to test their hypotheses, and create interactive models that demonstrate potential solutions. The assessment measures not their ability to memorize the scientific method but their capacity to apply it creatively to address authentic problems.

In these redefined assessments, AI isn't something students are prohibited from using. It's an essential tool they're expected to leverage skillfully and ethically. The focus shifts from what students can produce independently to what they can accomplish as effective collaborators with AI.

Throughout this progression, note how the teacher's role evolves. Rather than simply deliver content, they become a designer of learning experiences, a facilitator of student inquiry, and a mentor guiding ethical AI use. They spend less time grading routine assignments and more time engaging with students' unique creative processes and critical thinking.

This isn't a distant future! All these applications are possible with technology available today. But achieving this vision requires more than just access to AI tools. It requires a framework for thoughtful implementation that progressively renovates the education model instead of simply digitizing traditional practices.

REMOVING BARRIERS TO CREATION

Another transformative aspect of AI is its ability to remove technical barriers that have traditionally limited student creation. When properly integrated through the SAMR framework, AI enables students to express their ideas and demonstrate their understanding in ways that were previously impossible for all but the most technically skilled.

Consider the student who has brilliant ideas for stories but struggles with the mechanics of writing. With AI as a thought partner and editor, they can focus on developing characters and plot while the AI helps structure sentences and paragraphs. The result isn't an AI-generated story; it's the student's original vision, made accessible through technological assistance.

Or think about the student who wants to create a game to teach younger children about ecology but has no coding experience. Using AI to translate her concepts into functional code, she can design engaging gameplay and accurate content rather than get stuck on syntax errors. The technical barrier falls away, allowing her to create something that would have been unimaginable before.

This isn't about making things "easier" in the sense of lowering standards. It's about elevating what's possible by removing artificial constraints. Just as calculators freed mathematics students to focus on concepts rather than computation, AI frees learners to focus on higher-order thinking rather than technical execution. More on that in the "Create" chapter.

IT'S ABOUT ELEVATING WHAT'S POSSIBLE BY REMOVING ARTIFICIAL CONSTRAINTS.

PERSONALIZING LEARNING AT SCALE

Perhaps the most revolutionary potential of AI in education is its ability to make truly personalized learning accessible to all students, not just those in privileged settings with low student-to-teacher ratios.

At the redefinition level, AI becomes a tireless learning companion that adapts to each student's needs, interests, and learning patterns. It provides immediate, specific feedback on writing, adjusts the difficulty of problems based on performance, suggests relevant resources when a student is stuck, and even detects early signs of confusion or disengagement.

Meanwhile, teachers gain unprecedented insight into how their students learn. Rather than simply see what answers students got right or wrong, they can analyze patterns of thinking, identify specific misconceptions, and understand exactly where and why a student is struggling. This allows for targeted intervention that would be impossible even in the smallest of classes without AI assistance.

The result is a learning environment where every student receives the support they need, precisely when and how they need it. The one-size-fits-all approach that has dominated education for centuries gives way to learning experiences that adapt to individual needs while still building toward common goals.

However, some students may *not* want to utilize an AI tool this way. Especially at the university level, students want to receive instruction, remediation, and mentorship from real people: professors, faculty, teaching assistants, and tutors. AI can help build a learning environment in which every student receives the support they need—including the ones who would prefer to ask questions of a chatbot instead of raising their hand in class.

AI OPTIMISM: A NEW EDUCATIONAL PARADIGM

The examples we've explored aren't just isolated success stories—they're glimpses into a fundamentally different vision of education. One where technology amplifies human potential instead of replacing it. One where personalization isn't a luxury but a standard. One where barriers that have limited students for generations suddenly dissolve.

AI optimism is an approach grounded in possibility rather than panic, in agency rather than inevitability. It's distinct from both the reflexive fear that dominates many educational discussions about AI and the uncritical enthusiasm that overlooks legitimate concerns. To be AI optimistic is to acknowledge the valid concerns around privacy, equity, and ethics while refusing to let those concerns become paralyzing. Moving forward cautiously is better than standing still, and it's certainly better than pushing against.

> **AI OPTIMISM IS AN APPROACH GROUNDED IN POSSIBILITY RATHER THAN PANIC, IN AGENCY RATHER THAN INEVITABILITY.**

My optimism is grounded in the SAMR framework, which offers a pathway to move from simply using AI to automate existing practices (substitution) toward creating entirely new educational possibilities (redefinition). This framework acknowledges that meaningful transformation doesn't happen overnight but progresses through stages of implementation, with each stage building on the previous one.

In my work with educators around the world, I've witnessed how this perspective shift changes everything. Teachers who approach AI with optimism don't ask, "How do I prevent students from using AI?" but rather, "How do I use AI to deepen learning?" They don't focus solely on what might go wrong but actively explore what could go right. They see AI not as a threat to their professional identity but as an amplifier of their human capacities, like intuition, empathy, creativity, and judgment.

Of course, we must recognize barriers. We must address issues of AI literacy, equity of access, resource consumption, data privacy, and systemic resistance to change. Educational systems designed around standardized assessment and content coverage must evolve to value the creative, critical, and collaborative capabilities that AI helps develop.

The AI optimist recognizes that technology has always presented both risks and opportunities and that our choices shape which of those gets the most attention. An optimistic stance doesn't dismiss concerns. Instead, it approaches them as problems to be solved rather than reasons to avoid engagement.

Unlike previous technological revolutions in education, the barriers to AI adoption are primarily conceptual and cultural, not technical. Many of the tools are already widely available. What we need now is a framework to guide their implementation and help move innovation incrementally—and that's exactly what SAMR provides.

I invite you to adopt this lens of AI optimism. Let's explore AI's educational potential with both enthusiasm and discernment. The SAMR framework offers us a path to progress from basic AI implementations to truly transformative possibilities that turn education into something better, more equitable, and more aligned with the world our students will inherit.

In the next chapter, we'll explore the first steps of this journey, examining the practical foundations of AI implementation through prompting, ethical considerations, and tool selection.

FIRST STEPS

THE SAMR MODEL ENCOURAGES EDUCATORS to move beyond merely using technology as a substitute for traditional tools and toward learning experiences that were previously impossible. You don't have to be an early adopter, technology champion, or tech-savvy teacher to get started. SAMR offers us a powerful conceptual tool for understanding and choosing the best strategies for tech integration. It makes sense, then, to frame AI tools with this model. SAMR can be a framework to guide teachers in implementing AI in ways that truly shift education.

THE JOURNEY AHEAD

Before we dive into the specific applications of AI across the SAMR spectrum, let's map out how the pieces of this puzzle fit together. In the coming chapters, we'll explore six key educational processes where AI can make a profound impact:

1. **Design:** We begin with planning and designing learning experiences and systems. This is where the foundations are laid for everything that follows.
2. **Create:** Next comes developing the actual content, materials, and resources that students will engage with.
3. **Support:** This crucial phase focuses on implementing and supporting the learning process, ensuring students have the tools and assistance they need to succeed. While technically part of implementation, effective support must be planned from the

beginning, which is a key principle of Universal Design for Learning (UDL).
4. **Analyze:** As students engage with content and activities, we gather and analyze data to understand their progress, challenges, and needs. This happens during the learning process, allowing for real-time adjustments.
5. **Evaluate:** After implementation, we assess outcomes and effectiveness, looking at the bigger picture of what worked, what didn't, and why.
6. **Manage:** Throughout all these processes, we must handle the administrative and organizational aspects of education. While perhaps less exciting than other elements, effective management creates space for innovation to flourish.

These processes form a cycle rather than a strict linear progression. Analysis might lead us back to redesigning certain elements, evaluation might inspire new creative approaches, and management happens continuously. In each chapter, we'll explore how AI applications progress through the substitution, augmentation, and modification levels of SAMR, seeing practical examples for teachers, students, and administrators.

Why organize the book this way rather than present each SAMR level in its own chapter? Because real educational transformation doesn't happen all at once. You might be using AI at the redefinition level for design but the substitution level for evaluation. This approach allows you to see the full spectrum of possibilities in each area and choose your entry points strategically. And remember, I've reserved the redefinition level for its own chapter at the end because true redefinition often cuts across these categories, creating entirely new educational paradigms.

Before we get there, though, there are three essential foundations to establish for any AI implementation: practical application through informed praxis, navigating privacy considerations, and effective prompting.

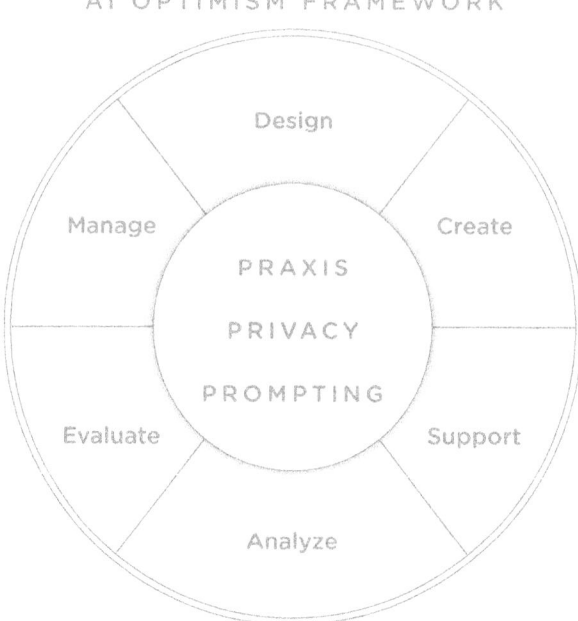

PRAXIS

Praxis is the beautiful intersection where theory meets practice—it's not just knowing something or just doing something but the thoughtful integration of both. In education, praxis means we don't just understand pedagogical theories; we actively apply them in our classrooms while continuously reflecting on and refining our practice based on what we learn from our students and our experiences.

When it comes to teaching with AI, praxis becomes even more critical. It's not enough to simply know that AI tools exist or to blindly implement them because they're trendy. True praxis with AI means understanding the theoretical foundations of how learning happens, recognizing how AI tools can enhance or transform that process, and then thoughtfully applying these tools while constantly evaluating their impact on student learning.

This is exactly what the SAMR model helps us achieve. It provides the theoretical framework for understanding how technology integration can progress from simple substitution to true transformation, but it only becomes meaningful when we put it into practice with real students in real classrooms and reflect on what works and what doesn't.

Throughout this book, I'm advocating for a praxis approach to AI in education. We can't just adopt AI tools because they save us time (though that's nice), and we can't dismiss them because they make us uncomfortable. Instead, we need to understand both the pedagogical principles that guide effective teaching and the capabilities of AI tools, then bring them together in ways that genuinely improve learning outcomes for our students. This means being intentional about when and how we use AI, continuously reflecting on its impact, and adjusting our approach based on what we observe. It's the difference between being a thoughtful educator who uses AI as a powerful tool for learning and being someone who either avoids AI entirely or uses it without considering its educational implications.

One of the biggest considerations around praxis right now is how students responsibly use AI. This isn't just about preventing plagiarism; it's about developing a thoughtful, intentional approach to AI that combines understanding with ethical practice. If prompting is focused on the input, then responsible AI use is focused on the relationship between the human and the tool throughout the entire process.

The plagiarism conversation has been a hot topic in education for a very long time. I remember carefully rephrasing sections of the encyclopedia for my primary school research projects and being worried my teacher would be angry that I traced the map of Africa to shade in where elephants lived. Then came the internet, and suddenly everyone had the ability to copy and paste large amounts of information.

When I was teaching middle school language arts, I'd often wonder whether sentences in my learners' writing were plagiarized. To check, I'd copy a sentence into a search engine and see if I got an exact hit. I once discovered a student had copied large sections of text from an online source without any citation, and I brought the concern to her parents. They were adamant that their twelve-year-old was such an excellent writer that she had somehow written the exact same ten sentences as an online source. I explained the likelihood of that happening was infinitesimal, but even after reviewing the highlighted sections of her paper and the website in front of them, they claimed she had written it herself. I can only imagine how passionately parents like those would defend a student who uses untraceable generative-writing supports. This kind of experience is exactly why we need to shift from a plagiarism-focused mindset to a praxis-focused approach with generative AI in schools.

Math teachers have been developing this kind of praxis for years with calculators. Once calculators became ubiquitous, the conversation shifted from *whether* learners should be allowed to use them to *when* learners should be allowed to use them—and how we could help them do so responsibly and effectively. The same evolution needs to happen with generative AI. We must shift from considering banning generative AI to assuming learners will use it and need to be taught how and when it's appropriate to do so. And we must understand not just the rules but the reasoning behind thoughtful use.

Right now, schools and educators are rushing to create simple AI policies that look like traffic lights: green for "AI allowed," yellow for "proceed with caution," and red for "absolutely no AI." These cut-and-dry rules might feel reassuring to administrators, but they put teachers at the center of every decision and rob students of the opportunity to develop their own judgment.

When we create rigid matrices that tell students exactly when they can and can't use AI, we're essentially saying, "Don't think about this—just follow the rules." But here's the problem: the real world doesn't work that way. In their future careers, our students won't have a laminated chart posted on the wall telling them whether they can use AI for a particular task. They need to develop critical thinking skills to make these decisions themselves.

A praxis approach means we're not just creating policies about AI use but helping students develop critical thinking skills to make good decisions about when and how to use these tools. We're modeling transparency about our own AI use and helping students understand the difference between AI as a thinking partner versus a way to avoid thinking altogether. Instead of being the AI police, we can become AI mentors. We can shift our focus from control to coaching. Rather than telling students, "You can't use AI for this assignment," we can teach them to ask themselves a simple but powerful question: "Does this use of AI limit my learning?"

This single question cuts through all the complexity of AI policies and gets to the heart of what education is about. When a student is tempted to use AI to write their entire essay, they can pause and ask: "Does this limit my learning?" Thinking about the answer will help them understand that yes, if AI does all the thinking and writing, they will miss out on developing their own critical thinking, voice, and writing skills. But if that same student wants to use AI to brainstorm ideas when they're stuck or to help organize their thoughts, the answer might be different. AI might enhance their learning by helping them overcome writer's block and focus on developing their ideas rather than struggling with where to start.

The real beauty of this question is that it puts the decision-making power back where it belongs: with the learner. It teaches them to think about the purpose of each assignment and how different tools might help or hinder their growth. Sometimes they'll make mistakes in their judgment, and that's part of the learning process too.

This doesn't mean we abandon all structure or guidance. We can create learning environments where students can practice making good decisions about AI use, reflect on the outcomes, and develop their own internal compass for responsible use. We can help students understand the purpose behind each learning experience and how different tools—including AI—might help or hinder that purpose, and we can model this thinking ourselves: "I'm going to use AI to help me create a first draft of this parent newsletter because the learning goal here isn't for me to practice my writing skills—it's to communicate effectively with families. But I wouldn't use AI to write feedback on your essays because my learning goal there is to understand your thinking and provide personalized guidance."

My favorite statement about this approach comes from the International Baccalaureate's "Statement from the IB about ChatGPT and Artificial Intelligence in Assesment and Education," published on March 1, 2023. It states:

> Latest developments in artificial intelligence (AI) software, such as ChatGPT, that can write sophisticated essay responses have generated a great deal of interest and discussion. The IB will not ban the use of AI software. The simplest reason is that it is an ineffective way to deal with innovation. However, the use of AI tools should be in line with the IB's academic integrity policy. We expect all our schools to discuss the various types of academic misconduct with their students.

This represents exactly the kind of praxis thinking we need—acknowledging the reality of the technology while maintaining our commitment to learning and integrity, and trusting educators and students to engage in meaningful conversations about appropriate use.

Individual educators and institutions should determine how generative AI fits into their academic integrity policy and communicate the guidelines to learners and families. But more than that, we need to help students develop their own internal compass for responsible AI use, guided by that essential question: "Does this limit my learning?"

Here are a few reflection questions to guide this important praxis development:

- How does generative AI fit into our existing academic integrity policy?
- How do we need to update the academic integrity policy to include generative AI?
- When do we expect educators to acknowledge their use of generative AI?

- When do we expect learners to acknowledge their use of generative AI?
- How will we communicate when generative AI is an appropriate support tool for an assignment?
- Are there instances where generative AI will be allowed in different ways for different learners?
- How will we intentionally guide learners in the appropriate use of generative AI?
- How will we provide education on critical thinking, ethics, privacy, and other citizenship topics with generative AI to our learners and their home support systems?

The goal isn't to create a perfect set of rules that prevent all misuse, it's to develop learners who can think critically about their choices and use AI in ways that enhance rather than replace their learning. When students internalize the question "Does this limit my learning?" they become partners in their own education rather than passive recipients of rules and restrictions.

> The key to successful AI implementation isn't technical expertise. It's curiosity, creativity, and a willingness to experiment. Start small, learn as you go, and remember that every educational innovation begins with someone willing to try something new.

PRIVACY

Throughout this book, I'll provide examples of how you can use generative AI in various educational contexts. Your experience might vary based on the specific tools you choose. While I'll test prompts across multiple platforms before sharing them, you should always adapt these examples to suit your preferred tools and context.

When using AI tools, it's vital to understand their data practices, especially when working with student information. Here are the key considerations:

Training data	Most generative AI models are trained on vast data sets collected from the internet and other sources. When you input text into these systems, your data may be stored and potentially used to train future versions of the model. This raises important questions about ownership and the life cycle of information you share.
Data retention	Different platforms have vastly different policies. Google Gemini, for example, might store your chat data for up to three years and make it available for human review, even if you delete your account. Microsoft Copilot for businesses and schools, on the other hand, keeps your chat data secured so that only you can ever see it. Always check the privacy policy and terms of service for any AI tool you plan to use with students.
Digital footprints	Every interaction with AI platforms creates a digital footprint that can be difficult or impossible to fully erase. Before sharing sensitive content, consider whether you'd be comfortable having this information permanently associated with you or your students.
Intellectual property	When we input prompts or upload content to AI systems, the outputs may exist in a gray area of intellectual property law. Some platforms explicitly claim rights to use outputs generated through their services, while others allow users to retain ownership. This becomes particularly important when creating original educational materials.
Equity concerns	Privacy considerations are inherently equity issues. Students from marginalized communities often face greater surveillance and data collection risks while having less power to advocate for their digital rights. When implementing AI, we must ensure that our privacy practices don't disproportionately impact already vulnerable populations.

PROTECTING PERSONAL DATA

Exercise extreme caution when considering using AI tools to help assess student work, write emails to families, or process other sensitive content like individual education plans (IEPs). Here are some general guidelines:

AVOID PERSONAL IDENTIFIERS: Never include student names, ID numbers, or other personally identifiable information in prompts.

DE-IDENTIFY EXAMPLES: If you need AI assistance with student work, remove all identifying information first and consider altering specific details.

USE EDUCATION-SPECIFIC TOOLS: When available, choose AI platforms specifically designed for educational use, as these typically offer stronger privacy protections and compliance with education privacy laws like FERPA.

VERIFY COMPLIANCE: Ensure any tool you adopt has been vetted and approved by your school or district's IT department and complies with relevant data privacy regulations.

MODEL APPROPRIATE USE: Teach students about responsible AI use, including how to protect their own privacy when using these tools.

EVALUATING AI TOOLS

Throughout this book, I provide concrete examples from my personal experience implementing AI tools in educational settings. Many of these examples feature Microsoft tools, reflecting my background and the environments where I've taught and worked. However, I want to emphasize that the principles and approaches discussed apply regardless of which specific tools you have available. Whether your school uses iPads, Chromebooks, Windows devices, or a mix of technologies and platforms, you'll find similar AI capabilities available.

The specific apps and tools mentioned are not endorsements but rather illustrations to make concepts tangible. I encourage you to explore equivalent options available in your technology ecosystem. The power of the SAMR framework is that it focuses on how we use technology rather than which technology we use. As you read, consider how you might apply these ideas using the specific tools accessible in your educational context. What matters most is not the platform but the thoughtful integration of AI to enhance teaching and learning.

Do your due diligence before adopting any platform for classroom use. Organizations like CoSN (Consortium for School Networking) and ISTE (International Society for Technology in Education) offer valuable resources to help evaluate educational technology from privacy and security perspectives.

Consider these questions when evaluating an AI tool:

- Who owns the data input into the system?
- How long is data retained?
- Is data used to train AI models?
- Is the platform compliant with relevant education privacy laws?
- Can data be permanently deleted if requested?
- How are student users protected if the tool is used in classrooms?

My goal in these pages is to give educators and system leaders guidance on implementing AI to positively impact student learning. The specific tools mentioned will inevitably evolve and change—sometimes rapidly. Focus on the principles and approaches rather than specific platforms, and always prioritize student privacy and data security in your decisions.

As we move into the next chapter and begin exploring specific applications of AI through the SAMR framework, keep these privacy considerations in mind. They form an essential foundation for ethical and responsible AI implementation in any educational context.

PROMPTING

Prompting, or prompt engineering, is a technique used to effectively communicate with generative AI systems like chatbots or language models. It involves crafting specific questions or directions, known as prompts, that guide the AI to produce the desired output. For educators, mastering prompt engineering is essential to leveraging AI as a tool for teaching and learning. You don't need a paid subscription to a tool claiming to do it all; you just need to know how to write prompts.

My journey with prompt engineering began quite unexpectedly. After experimenting with ChatGPT for a few weeks, I realized my results varied wildly. Sometimes I got exactly what I needed, but other times I received responses that missed my point entirely (of course, this was early on, and the models have improved greatly since then). I started keeping a prompt journal, documenting which phrasings worked best for different tasks. I just used Notepad on my PC so I could copy and paste out of it easily whenever needed.

This skill was put to the test when I was asked to create a professional development session on AI literacy for elementary educators. Obviously, this is a topic I believe in deeply, but at the time, I hadn't formally presented on it yet. With a limited amount of time to prepare, I needed to quickly gather age-appropriate examples, create hands-on activities, and design follow-up resources. Instead of spending hours searching for classroom applications, I crafted a detailed prompt requesting developmentally appropriate AI literacy activities that aligned with existing K–5 digital citizenship frameworks. I had to use a model with web grounding because there wasn't much of this in the data set used by other apps! After refining the prompt to include specific requirements for activities that wouldn't need advanced technology, I had a set of practical classroom exercises that built critical-thinking skills around AI concepts like data, patterns, and algorithmic bias.

What impressed me most was how effective prompting changed my preparation process. For the hands-on portion of the workshop, I created a prompt that generated a decision-making scenario where teacher teams would evaluate child-friendly AI tools using an assessment framework we developed together. The AI tool produced thoughtful evaluation criteria that considered ethical implications, privacy concerns, and pedagogical value while remaining accessible to teachers with varying technical backgrounds. Several participants later told me it was the most practical technology PD they'd experienced. I realized then that skillful prompting wasn't just saving me time. It was elevating the quality of my work in ways I hadn't anticipated.

None of this is magic. It's code and algorithms and predictive patterns. Special tools designed for educators will help by setting specific parameters on your behalf, and that's a great way to learn when you first get started. But I hope that you take the time to use these prescriptive tools as an opportunity to learn how prompting works, and then you customize, remix, and repurpose the prompts in any generative AI app.

I try to model different tools within this book, and I use a variety of LLMs in my daily life. My goal is to empower you to use them in a way that goes beyond an "easy button." Here are some things to keep in mind when you're engineering prompts:

> **UNDERSTAND THE MODEL:** Recognize that AI models have been trained on vast amounts of data and generate responses based on the prompts they receive. Different models respond differently, just like different people answer the same question in unique ways. Each prompt will return a unique response, and asking the same question again will generate something new, though it may follow similar patterns.

USE CLARITY AND SPECIFICITY: The more precise your prompt, the more relevant and accurate your response will be. Instead of asking "How do I teach math?" try "What are some effective strategies for teaching algebra to high school learners who struggle with abstract concepts?" AI uses predictive analytics (like predictive text on your phone) to craft responses. More details in your prompt provide more patterns for analysis, typically resulting in more useful responses.

PREPARE FOR AN ITERATIVE PROCESS: Prompt engineering isn't a one-shot deal. It often requires refining your prompts based on initial responses. This iterative approach leads to better results over time as you learn what works. Don't be afraid to follow up with requests for simplification, elaboration, or a different approach.

RETAIN CONTEXTUAL AWARENESS: AI uses the entire conversation to generate responses. This means you can build on previous exchanges without repeating information. If you're in the same conversation, you can ask for more details, different perspectives, or new ideas related to the topic. Some models also allow you to reference external information, like files or saved preferences.

CONSIDER ETHICAL ASPECTS: When crafting prompts, consider the ethical implications of your requests. Be thoughtful about sharing personally identifiable information, student work, or sensitive content. Different platforms have varying data retention policies: Google Gemini stores your chat data for years (even if you delete your account) and makes it available for human review, while enterprise-level platforms for businesses and schools keep your conversations private and accessible only to you.

Review the terms of use and privacy policies of any AI tool you use with students.

Also remember that AI models will choose to fabricate information (sometimes called hallucinations) before admitting uncertainty. Always verify important information, especially for historical facts, scientific data, or current events.

There are many frameworks for writing effective prompts, but most experts agree on several basic components. One framework I particularly like is Dr. Sabba Quidwai's SPARK model, which she's kindly allowed me to share here:

S IS FOR SITUATION: Describe the current context or setting that requires AI assistance.

P IS FOR PROBLEM: Clearly identify the challenge or issue that needs addressing.

A IS FOR ASPIRATIONS: Define the desired outcomes or goals you wish to achieve.

R IS FOR RESULTS: Specify the tangible benefits or changes you expect from using AI.

K IS FOR KISMET: Embrace the serendipitous discoveries or unexpected positive outcomes that can arise.

What makes SPARK particularly powerful is its emphasis on prompting humans first. You are the expert, so it's your responsibility (not magic!) to guide the process toward the outcomes you need and to check those outcomes for relevance, accuracy, bias, and purpose.

For example, an educator might write a prompt like this: "Create a set of engaging biology quiz questions for high school learners that cover the topic of photosynthesis, including diagrams that illustrate the process, and provide detailed explanations for each answer."

Let's break that down by its SPARK components:

First, the educator thinks through what they need to support an upcoming lesson, what it should include, and what's needed.

SITUATION: The educator needs to prepare a biology quiz.

PROBLEM: The quiz must be engaging and informative.

ASPIRATIONS: The goal is to enhance learners' understanding of photosynthesis.

RESULTS: The educator expects a set of well-crafted questions with diagrams and explanations.

KISMET: The potential is for learners to gain deeper insights and interest in biology through this quiz.

Finally, the educator checks the output and any sources listed and iterates or edits the content based on personal expertise.

This simple example illustrates how prompting can function at different levels of the SAMR model.

At the substitution level, the educator is using AI to generate quiz questions that they might have created manually before. The task itself, creating assessment questions, hasn't fundamentally changed, but the process is more efficient.

Moving to augmentation, notice how the prompt specifically requests diagrams and detailed explanations. These functional improvements enhance the educational value of the quiz beyond what the teacher might have easily created without AI assistance. Students receive visual representations and thorough explanations that support deeper understanding.

To reach modification, the educator might build on this foundation by prompting AI to create questions that incorporate real-world applications or that connect photosynthesis to current environmental issues. They could then use these questions not just for assessment but as discussion starters for collaborative problem-solving activities, significantly redesigning the learning task.

At the redefinition level, the educator might use AI to help students create their own interactive simulations of photosynthesis based on variables they want to test, or to design plant growth experiments that collect and analyze real-time data. This creates learning experiences that would have been impossible without technology.

This progression shows how even a simple prompt for quiz questions can be the starting point for a journey through the SAMR model, gradually altering both the teaching process and the learning experience.

Choose the prompting method that works best for you, the one you can use consistently and that seems to produce generally satisfactory results for the app you're using. Remember that apps respond differently to inputs, so you might need to try a different app or a different approach if you're not getting what you need even after careful prompting.

PART II
THE SAMR JOURNEY THROUGH EDUCATIONAL TASKS

5

DESIGN

EFFECTIVE DESIGN LIES AT THE heart of every successful learning experience and educational system. It's the blueprint phase where we plan structures, map pathways, and envision possibilities before any content creation begins. During design, educators outline units and lessons, students sketch project approaches, and administrators architect programs and initiatives.

The planning phase often presents challenges. New teachers frequently struggle to identify essential standards, establish appropriate pacing, differentiate for diverse learners, and structure engaging learning sequences. Students may have ambitious ideas but lack the frameworks to organize their thinking effectively. Administrators face designing systems that support varied learning needs while meeting organizational requirements.

Traditional approaches to educational design can be time-consuming and isolating. Teachers spend countless hours researching standards alignments and planning differentiated pathways. Students might struggle to organize complex projects without appropriate scaffolding. School leaders may find themselves overwhelmed when designing new programs amid competing priorities and constraints.

This is where artificial intelligence offers huge potential for everyone in the educational ecosystem. At the most basic level, AI can streamline routine planning tasks, giving educators, students, and administrators more time to focus on higher-value design decisions. As we move up the SAMR ladder, AI becomes a collaborative partner in designing innovative learning experiences that would have been impossible without technology's assistance.

This chapter focuses exclusively on the planning and organization phase of education. The actual creation of content, materials, and resources will be addressed in the next chapter. Here, we're concerned with the architectural blueprints, not the construction itself.

Through *substitution*, we'll see how AI can generate questions, surveys, discussion responses, and draft communications, saving time while maintaining the fundamental creation process.

In *augmentation*, we'll discover how AI-enhanced content generation adds functional improvements that make educational materials more engaging and effective.

At the *modification* level, we'll examine how AI significantly shifts creative tasks, enabling the development of interactive videos, personalized resources, and multimedia experiences that fundamentally change how students engage with content.

Whether you're a classroom teacher sketching out next quarter's curriculum, a student structuring an ambitious project, or a school leader designing institution-wide programs, this chapter offers practical ways to leverage AI in designing learning experiences and systems that are more engaging, inclusive, and effective for all.

> AI optimism in design isn't about replacing human creativity! It's about removing the barriers that have historically constrained it. Design needs human insight, empathy, and vision. The result isn't less human design but more deeply human design.

SUBSTITUTION

Project Plans

For many learners, starting a large project is a painful undertaking. We've all seen the outcomes of learners who don't start a project early and then panic toward the end. There are a plethora of memes and videos dedicated to the last-minute project completion, showing stress at home for both adults and children. Generative AI certainly can't make a student more disciplined, give them a longer attention span, or ensure they focus on a project. But it can help create a plan or schedule. Sometimes that's the hardest part. Let's give learners some assistance in creating their baby-steps plan and a schedule to meet their needs and work style.

> **SAMPLE PROMPT**
>
> I am a sixth-grade student. I have a project for my coding and design class. I have to develop a product that meets the needs of a specific audience. I have to follow the design thinking steps. I need help creating a schedule. First help me by creating a list of things I need to do to be successful in this project. Then create a schedule of action items that shows step by step how to complete each part of the project. This project is three weeks long and I'd like to work on it every day but not on weekends. I'd like to see the schedule in a table or chart.

When learners are using generative AI to support their project planning, consider using chain-of-thought (CoT) prompting. This method involves generating intermediate steps or explanations that mimic human reasoning when solving complex problems. Benefits of CoT prompting include the following:

STEP-BY-STEP REASONING: Instead of providing an answer directly, the model breaks down the problem into smaller, manageable steps, explaining each part of the thought process. This approach is similar to how a person might work through a math problem by writing down each calculation before arriving at the final answer.

IMPROVED ACCURACY: By breaking down the reasoning process, CoT prompting helps reduce errors that might arise from oversimplification or misinterpretation of the problem. This detailed approach often leads to more accurate and reliable results.

TRANSPARENCY AND INTERPRETABILITY: CoT prompting makes the model's decision-making process more transparent and interpretable. Users can follow the reasoning to understand how the conclusion was reached.

CoT prompting can be particularly useful in areas like mathematical problem-solving, logical reasoning tasks, complex decision-making, and explaining scientific concepts. It can also enhance the model's ability to provide detailed explanations and justifications for its responses. To generate these types of outputs, include terms like *step-by-step* in the prompt. It's perfect for making a project plan.

Working with Standards

The first time I asked generative AI to take a lesson I'd written and tell me which standards it aligned to, I was floored by the results. What would have taken me at least an hour of combing through Common Core took seconds. Now, many teachers know the standards for their primary content area backward and forward, which is a good thing. But cross-curricular connections, which are so important in education, are a burden to find for teachers unfamiliar with them. If I am a language arts teacher working on a writing lesson plan for a literacy project, I might want to integrate social studies or science standards. Finding the appropriate standards is time-consuming for me as a human, but it's quick for a GPT that already has the data categorized, organized, and coded.

Make sure to ask the GPT for the specific standards you need to align to, by subject and grade level. The data set includes education standards from around the world, so being vague may return unusable results. You can simply copy and paste the lesson into the GPT, upload your lesson file, or open a lesson on a public web page.

> **SAMPLE PROMPT**
>
> Identify NGSS standards for middle school learners that are covered in this lesson. Explain how each standard is met in the lesson.

I find that adding the explanation is a built-in fact-checker for me. I will need to confirm the standards are correct, but this is much quicker if AI has provided the explanation. When an explanation is fabricated, it's easier to identify that by reading the explanation.

This approach also works in the other direction. We can ask generative AI to develop class activities, tasks, assessments, and even full lesson plans based on a set of standards. Some apps allow you to generate entire presentations from a single standard!

The longer the output you're aiming for, the more information you should include in the prompt. For example, a list of three science experiments for a particular science standard is simple enough to generate. But a full lesson plan for a science concept requires more expertise. You may need the lesson plan in a particular format. You may have a time period requirement or need to include accommodations.

> **SAMPLE PROMPT 1**
>
> I am teaching a current events lesson to my civics class. What are five topics we could use to break into small groups and discuss?

> **SAMPLE PROMPT 2**
>
> I am teaching variables to my computer science beginning coders. What is a hands-on, unplugged, interactive activity we could do together to introduce variables?

> **SAMPLE PROMPT 3**
>
> I am teaching a lesson on digital footprints to my second-grade learners. I need to communicate this topic in a way they will understand. I like to begin these lessons with a read aloud to build schema and interest. Then we complete an unplugged activity for about ten minutes, then a digital activity for about twenty minutes. We end with a reflection time together for about five minutes. I have one hour to teach this entire lesson. Write a lesson plan that includes materials, lesson introduction, student group work, student independent work, and assessment. I have one student who will need accommodations for a visual impairment.

While AI-generated lesson plans kick-start creativity, bring fresh ideas, and save time in content creation, they need to be carefully reviewed by the expert (you, the human) before they're implemented with learners. I was a little surprised to see a recent example using generative AI to create a lesson script. Unless you're completely unfamiliar with the content, I don't recommend that. Use caution when generating student-facing content, especially full lesson plans. You may need to make many changes, but the benefit is in being given a starting point and building upon it with your own customizations.

> Remember that meaningful change doesn't happen overnight. Each time you substitute a routine task with AI assistance, you're building the skills and confidence to eventually transform your practice into more powerful outputs.

AUGMENTATION

Mind Mapping

Mind mapping is a powerful tool for brainstorming and organizing ideas, and with the integration of AI, it has become even more effective. Learners and educators have been using mind maps for a long time, but traditional mind mapping on paper has many disadvantages. On the other hand, digital mind mapping tools mean learners can rearrange, edit, sort, and search their notes. This helps organize thoughts even more efficiently. For example, when learners input their ideas into a mind map, AI can automatically categorize and cluster similar concepts, making it easier to see connections and identify key themes. This can save time during short class periods and enhance the clarity and structure of brainstorming sessions. Modern mind mapping tools like Padlet, Canva, and Miro now offer AI-powered features that sort and filter ideas, providing augmented support for learners during the ideation process.

Padlet's AI features, such as Magic Padlet, allow learners to generate and organize ideas quickly. The AI can create entire padlets based on a description, helping learners brainstorm and structure their ideas. For instance, if learners are working on a group project, they can use Padlet to generate discussion boards and idea lists together, then ask AI to organize the ideas into coherent categories.

Canva's Magic Studio offers a suite of AI tools that assist in the creative process. Learners can use Magic Design to generate custom content, including mind maps, based on their descriptions. The AI helps by suggesting key words, connecting ideas, and identifying gaps in the mind map. This makes the brainstorming process more dynamic and interactive, allowing learners to visualize their ideas more effectively. AI will also sort the notes on a whiteboard, similar to Padlet's functionality.

Miro's AI features enhance the brainstorming process by generating, summarizing, and clustering ideas based on sentiment and key words. This helps learners quickly organize their thoughts and focus on the most relevant concepts. Miro AI can also create visual representations of complex information, making it easier for learners to understand and communicate their own ideas.

AI-enhanced mind mapping tools augment traditional brainstorming by adding functional improvements like automatic sorting, searching, and color-coding that make the organization of ideas more efficient and effective. These capabilities enhance our ability to visualize connections while maintaining the core purpose of traditional mind mapping.

MODIFICATION

Course Catalog

Navigating the course catalog can be a daunting task for students, especially when they're trying to align their choices with academic goals, graduation requirements, and personal interests. A generative AI tool, such as a chatbot, can significantly ease this process by providing instant, tailored information about course offerings, prerequisites, and scheduling options.

A chatbot can serve as a virtual adviser, available 24/7 to answer questions that might otherwise overwhelm school counseling offices, especially during peak times like registration periods. Students can inquire about specific courses, ask for recommendations based on their interests or career goals, and even explore different academic pathways. And it's all through a user-friendly, conversational interface. This not only saves time for both students and counselors but also empowers students to take more ownership of their academic planning.

This use of a generative AI chatbot for course catalog assistance is an example of task modification rather than simple substitution because it fundamentally changes how the task is performed, offering capabilities that extend beyond merely automating an existing process.

Substitution would involve replacing a traditional method with a digital equivalent without changing the core nature of the task. For example, if a PDF version of the course catalog was simply made available online, that would be substitution; the information is the same, just in a different format. Modification, on the other hand, involves redesigning the task to leverage technology in a way that adds new value. In this case, the AI chatbot not only provides information from the course catalog but also enhances the process through personalization, interactivity, anytime access, and integrations.

The chatbot can offer tailored course recommendations based on individual student data such as academic performance, interests, and career aspirations. This level of personalized guidance is a step beyond what a static course catalog or even a basic digital version could provide. Students can engage in a dynamic conversation with the chatbot, asking follow-up questions, exploring different academic paths, and receiving real-time, context-aware responses. This interactive process is more engaging and informative than simply reading through a list of courses. Unlike traditional counseling services, the chatbot is available at any time, providing students with immediate support when they need it, even outside of school hours. This availability increases the accessibility and convenience of academic planning. I definitely would have appreciated a chatbot when I was helping my son pick out a college degree program late one night!

The chatbot can integrate with other school systems, pulling real-time data to provide the most up-to-date information, track student progress, and ensure that the advice given aligns with graduation requirements or other academic goals. This automation streamlines the process and reduces the administrative burden on human counselors. By adjusting the way students interact with the course catalog and receive academic guidance, the use of a generative AI chatbot exemplifies task modification, as it enhances and expands the original task in ways that were not possible before.

Several AI tools are well suited for this task. Platforms that allow you to build your own GPTs or chatbots can be programmed to analyze and respond to student queries about the course catalog. These tools can be integrated into a school's existing online systems, allowing students to seamlessly access information and receive personalized guidance based on their academic history and future goals. Additionally, enterprise-level offerings like Copilot Studio and ChatGPT Edu offer strong integration capabilities with a school's existing data, which can make it easier to deploy and maintain a course catalog chatbot tailored to the specific needs of a school.

> **SAMPLE PROMPT**
>
> Create a chatbot that assists high school students with course selection. The chatbot should be able to (1) provide information about available courses, including descriptions, prerequisites, and scheduling options; (2) offer personalized course recommendations based on the student's grade level, past academic performance, and career interests; (3) answer common questions about graduation requirements and how certain courses fit into those requirements; (4) allow students to compare different academic pathways, such as college prep; vocational training, or advanced placement options; and (5) integrate with the school's existing student information system to offer real-time, personalized advice. Use <file> as the course catalog.

You will need to use a GPT that accesses your data in real time, pulling from a file that includes all the course information. AI-powered course catalog chatbots modify the process of academic planning by changing what was once a static information lookup into an interactive, personalized guidance experience.

Culturally Responsive and Universally Designed Content

Speaking of creating content differently, we can shift our thinking from churning out cookie-cutter lessons from an AI tool to intentionally designing content with our learners in mind. This is a part of UDL, but it's also culturally responsive teaching, which focuses on providing multiple perspectives, teaching historical empathy, celebrating the agency and achievements of all, using a variety of visual and interactive materials, encouraging respectful classroom discussions from multiple perspectives, and connecting content to learners' cultural backgrounds and experiences. When designing AI-enhanced learning experiences, we must acknowledge that AI models may encode societal biases present in their training data. Creating truly equitable learning environments requires us to critically evaluate AI-generated content for representational gaps, stereotypes, or perspectives that might marginalize certain student groups.

AI can help educators create lesson plans that incorporate diverse perspectives and materials. For example, AI tools can suggest culturally relevant texts, examples, and case studies that reflect the backgrounds and experiences of all learners. AI can also analyze existing lesson plans and materials to identify potential biases or gaps in cultural representation. By evaluating the content, AI can suggest modifications to make lessons more inclusive. For instance, an AI tool could highlight areas where diverse voices are underrepresented and recommend additional resources or perspectives to include.

I tried the below sample prompt in six different GPTs, based on the demographics of my classroom when I taught US history to seventh-grade students in the Seattle area. I thought I would find a clear winner, but they were all completely different!

DESIGN | 61

> **SAMPLE PROMPT**
>
> I am a secondary educator getting ready to teach a unit to my history students about westward expansion. I have a range of students in my class: Black, White, Korean, Ukrainian, Indian, Mexican, and Russian. What are some culturally responsive resources I can use with my learners that reflect their backgrounds?

Given this sample prompt is about diverse perspectives, I think now is a good time to review the differences in the GPT responses.

Copilot gave me three direct links to resources and five strategies for culturally responsive teaching that were not specifically tied to the demographics I included in my prompt.

ChatGPT responded with categories of primary sources I could use, with examples by cultural background. It did not include any source links. It also included three activity suggestions and three suggested readings I could use that fit the cultural background of the students.

Poe gave me examples of primary sources, specific names of supplementary texts, three multimedia titles, and three instructional strategies.

Claude responded with ideas for each cultural group as well as how I could guide the students to find parallels and themes among their groups. It also recommended student projects.

Perplexity was the only tool to respond with imagery. It also provided a list of discussion topics to incorporate multiple perspectives, a short list of literature and film suggestions, and ways to increase student engagement.

Latimer was possibly the least helpful, offering one discussion topic per cultural group (but it combined Korean, Ukrainian, and Indian into one group) and a reminder to use literature, art, and music from diverse backgrounds.

If you're going to focus on modifying lesson plans (and changing tasks for learners) based on culturally responsive teaching, it might be a good idea to try a few different tools! AI tools for culturally responsive teaching change how educators develop an inclusive curriculum by enabling customization based on student demographics and unique classroom contexts. These tools help teachers create learning experiences that reflect diverse perspectives, ensuring materials connect authentically with students' backgrounds while remaining aligned with educational standards.

Immersive Spaces

There are several categories within immersive spaces that completely change the learning experience. AI can significantly enhance the use of AR, VR, and XR (augmented, virtual, and extended reality) in education by moving traditional tasks into immersive learning experiences. For instance, AI can tailor AR/VR/XR content to match each learner's pace and learning style. An AI-powered VR app like EON Reality can adjust the difficulty of a virtual lab experiment based on the learner's performance, providing hints and additional resources as needed. What's more, AI can provide immediate feedback during immersive experiences. In 2020, I visited the HoloLens immersive lab on the Microsoft campus and participated in an augmented reality simulation in which I had to fix a broken piece on an airplane. I fumbled a bit through the process (I'm not an airplane mechanic, after all!). I selected the wrong tools multiple times and attempted to remove parts in the incorrect sequence. Each mistake required me to restart that section of the repair, and I found myself spending more time on trial and error than actual learning. While I eventually completed the repair, I left with a fragmented understanding of aircraft maintenance principles rather than the comprehensive knowledge the simulation intended to provide.

Had AI-powered support been available at the time (it certainly is now), it could have changed this experience entirely. An AI assistant could have observed my attempts, identified my specific confusion points, and offered gradual support. Perhaps the assistant could have first suggested which tool category to consider, then provided more specific guidance if I continued to struggle. It could have explained the mechanical principles behind each step, helping me understand why certain actions were necessary instead of just walking through procedures. The AI might have adapted to my learning style, offering more visual cues when I seemed to respond better to them or providing more detailed explanations when I appeared confused by a particular concept.

Most importantly, instead of forcing me to restart after each mistake, AI could have turned those errors into learning opportunities by explaining what went wrong, why it mattered, and how to correct it. This would have created a more fluid, less frustrating experience where mistakes became valuable parts of the learning process rather than obstacles to it.

This combination of immersive technology and adaptive AI support can create something far more powerful than either component alone. It can create a truly personalized learning environment that adjusts in real time to the learner's needs, turning what might be a frustrating experience into an engaging, effective educational opportunity.

AI also enhances interactivity within AR/VR/XR environments. In a virtual biology lab, AI can simulate complex biological processes and allow learners to interact with them, manipulating DNA sequences or observing cellular functions up close. Platforms like ClassVR support these interactive experiences by overlaying digital elements onto real-world objects. ClassVR provides thousands of educational virtual and augmented reality resources to add value to lessons in a variety of subjects. AI can also analyze data from learners' interactions with these environments to create adaptive learning paths. This means that the content and challenges presented to learners can evolve based on their progress, ensuring a more personalized and effective learning journey.

Immersive simulations generated by AI provide learners with hands-on experience in a safe, controlled environment. For example, medical students can practice surgical procedures in a VR setting with AI providing guidance and assessing their performance. Collaborative learning is also facilitated by AI in virtual spaces. With platforms like

ENGAGE VR, learners can work together on projects in a shared VR environment, with AI mediating discussions, suggesting resources, and ensuring that each participant is engaged and contributing.

AI also assists in creating rich, immersive content for AR/VR/XR experiences. This includes generating realistic scenarios, dialogues, and environments that enhance the learning experience and make it more engaging. For example, while a learner navigates a virtual historical site using an app like Google Arts & Culture, AI can offer insights and quiz them on key facts, reinforcing learning in real time.

By integrating AI with AR, VR, and XR, educators can create completely new learning experiences that go beyond traditional methods, making education more interactive, personalized, and effective for all learners.

Unit Planning

Unit planning, an important but often burdensome aspect of effective teaching, can be significantly streamlined and enhanced with AI. In fact, AI offers educators the ability to create comprehensive, customized unit plans that align with educational standards and learning objectives, saving valuable time and effort.

For instance, TeachAid allows teachers to input specific topics, standards, and objectives and generate a detailed unit plan that includes lesson outlines, activities, assessments, and resources. This not only ensures that the curriculum is well structured and aligned with instructional goals but also provides a framework that can be easily adapted to meet the needs of diverse learners.

Moreover, AI can assist in generating ideas for curriculum unit outlines, rubrics for assessing student work, class discussion questions, and learning resources. What's different about a tool like TeachAid is its ability to modify the lesson plans, presentations, activities, and other downloadable exports when the teacher makes an adjustment to the unit plan. If the teacher adds or removes a standard, for example, the entire plan will regenerate based on this adjustment. The power of being able to modify the unit plan without starting from scratch is exciting for educators.

It would be difficult to achieve this level of application with a standard GPT. As more companies develop tools to help with teacher planning, we can expect to see more flexible, adaptable technologies appear on the education scene.

Infographics

Most learners, and even most educators, do not have great experience with graphic design. Unless you have a past career or technical education focus in graphic design, your creations can be limited and a time sink. This is why tools like Canva have been so incredibly popular in every industry. They help people with little to no design skills turn ideas into beautiful, professional graphics.

Generative AI can do this for your learners, which modifies the task from *creating an infographic* to *brainstorming great ideas*. If you've ever watched learners (or adults) spend *way* too long simply choosing a font in PowerPoint, you know what I mean. And if you feel like I do about Comic Sans in hot pink, you're definitely going to want to try this out with your students! Infographics can have a content focus, and they're a solid alternative to a presentation. Think PowerPoint's SmartArt but even more advanced.

To create a quality infographic, learners need to focus on the following:

Critical thinking		Designing infographics requires students to analyze and synthesize information, helping them develop critical-thinking skills.
Information organization		Infographics help students organize information logically, making complex data more accessible and understandable.
Research skills		The process of creating infographics encourages students to improve their research skills, including finding and evaluating trustworthy sources.
Tech literacy		Infographic creation meets technology literacy standards because students use digital tools to design and present their work.
Creativity		Infographics allow students to express their understanding creatively, combining text, images, and data in visually appealing ways.
Engagement		Visual elements in infographics can increase student engagement and motivation, making learning more interactive and enjoyable.
Memory retention		Visual aids like infographics can enhance memory retention, as students are more likely to remember visual information compared to text alone.
Communication skills		Creating infographics helps students improve their ability to communicate complex ideas clearly and concisely.
Cultural responsiveness		Infographics can be tailored to include culturally relevant content, making learning more inclusive and relatable for diverse student populations.

If a learner uses an AI-powered infographic maker, which of these skills are they practicing? All of them! They still need to input information, edit the output, make decisions about the design, review and revise, approve, publish, and possibly present their work. One huge benefit is that the outcome isn't entirely dependent on a learner's design skills. By scaffolding their thinking and ideas with AI design, we remove many barriers.

Let's say a younger student is learning basic facts about the solar system. They begin by reading, watching a video, or participating in a virtual field trip. Using an AI-powered infographic tool (Piktochart AI is a good one, or give Napkin a try!), the learner inputs the topic "solar system" and provides some key points they want included, such as the names and order of the planets, their distances from the sun, and unique features of each planet. The AI creates a visually appealing infographic template. The learner then customizes the design by adding images of planets, using different colors to represent different types of planets (e.g., gas planets versus terrestrial planets) and adding some of their favorite facts about each one. The learner then reviews the content for accuracy and clarity. They might also add interactive elements in a tool like Genially or ThingLink. Finally, they share their infographic with the class.

I love this lesson because it integrates technology with core learning objectives, making the whole experience more engaging. Learners can focus on the content and critical-thinking aspects of the task instead of getting bogged down by a design challenge. Educators can focus on research, organization, and digital literacy while giving space for creativity and personal customization.

CONCLUSION

I hope after reading through this chapter you can see how artificial intelligence is positively impacting the design process in education. What began as simple substitution—using AI to generate project outlines or align standards—quickly expanded into powerful augmentation and modification of how we plan and structure learning experiences.

For teachers, AI tools help move curriculum planning from a solitary, research-intensive process into a guided, creative endeavor where routine organizational tasks are handled efficiently, leaving more energy for instructional architecture. For students, these same tools provide frameworks that enable more ambitious, well-structured project planning while still honoring their unique visions. For administrators and school leaders, AI offers ways to design comprehensive program structures that address diverse needs while maintaining coherence.

When implemented thoughtfully through the SAMR framework, AI doesn't replace anyone's design expertise. It amplifies our expertise! The tools and approaches we've discussed allow you to focus on the strategic aspects of design that require human creativity, empathy, and wisdom.

Perhaps most importantly, AI makes possible design practices that would otherwise be unrealistic for any individual to accomplish. Planning truly personalized learning pathways, designing universal access frameworks, or mapping immersive learning sequences would traditionally require extensive specialist input and countless planning hours. With AI assistance, these approaches become accessible to anyone in the educational community willing to learn the tools.

The SAMR framework reminds us that the goal isn't simply to use AI, but to use it in ways that reimagine both our design processes and the resulting educational blueprints. As you implement these ideas in classroom curricula, student projects, or school-wide initiatives, consider not just how AI can help you design faster but how it can help you design differently. It can help create frameworks and structures that would have been impossible before.

In the next chapter, we'll move from design to creation, exploring how AI can support the development of actual content, materials, and resources that bring these designs to life. While design provides the blueprint, creation gives it substance and form.

6

CREATE

CREATING EDUCATIONAL CONTENT IS BOTH an art and a science. For many teachers, it's a blend of creativity, expertise, and responsiveness to student needs. Yet in the reality of today's educational burdens, this creative work often gets compressed by time constraints and overwhelming demands. Tired teachers find themselves relying on generic worksheets from unvetted websites, reusing the same presentations year after year or crafting rushed assessments late into the evening. Students, facing tight deadlines and unclear expectations, may fall into predictable patterns of "just get it done" for their projects. Administrators, juggling many responsibilities, struggle to make their communications stand out amid information overload.

These challenges aren't due to lack of creativity or commitment. They're the natural result of systems that demand more content than any individual can reasonably produce with limited time and resources. Even the most innovative educators can find themselves making compromises, knowing they could create more engaging, personalized materials if only they had more hours in the day.

This is precisely where artificial intelligence offers such exciting potential. AI doesn't replace the human creativity that makes education meaningful. It amplifies it. AI handles routine aspects of content generation while freeing people to focus on the elements that require human insight, empathy, and vision. The most inspiring educators have always found ways to break out of routine, take ownership of what they create, and craft memorable learning experiences.

As we explore creation with AI, we inevitably encounter challenging questions about acceptable use. The educational community's initial response has centered on concerns about "AI cheating," leading to fear, shame, and outright bans in many settings. This narrow focus misses the opportunity before us. Instead of policing the boundaries of what we consider cheating, we might better serve our learners by asking what new possibilities AI can unlock.

Whether you're a teacher seeking to break out of content-creation routines, a student looking to find your authentic voice, or an administrator working to craft communications that truly resonate, this chapter offers practical ways to leverage AI to create materials that inspire, engage, and empower. With AI handling routine aspects of creation, everyone can take greater pride and ownership in what they produce—with just a little assistance.

Through *substitution*, we'll see how AI can assist with generating questions, surveys, discussion responses, and draft communications, saving valuable time while maintaining the fundamental creation process.

In *augmentation*, we'll discover how AI-enhanced content generation adds functional improvements that make educational materials more engaging and effective.

At the *modification* level, we'll examine how AI significantly enhances creative tasks, enabling the development of interactive videos, personalized resources, and multimedia experiences that fundamentally change how students engage with content.

Remember that all creation builds upon the designs explored in the previous chapter. While design provides the blueprint, creation gives it substance and form. With AI as your collaborative partner, you can bring your educational visions to life in ways that were previously impossible due to time, technical constraints, or other limitations.

> The AI optimist sees content creation not as a competition where either humans or machines come out on top, but as a collaborative partnership that amplifies human potential. Let's shift our perspective from viewing AI as a competitor to seeing it as a creative agent. You might find some of the most meaningful, engaging, and personalized educational content emerges at the intersection of human imagination and technological possibilities.

SUBSTITUTION

Create Questions for Quizzes or Discussions

Creating effective quiz and discussion questions is a cornerstone of teaching, and it's one that demands significant time and creativity. Week after week, sometimes day after day, educators need questions that accurately assess understanding, promote critical thinking, and align with learning standards. Even the most experienced teachers can find themselves falling into predictable question patterns or spending evenings crafting assessments instead of focusing on other aspects of teaching. This is where AI offers immediate, practical support. By generating varied question sets based on any content you provide, AI can break up question-writing routines, ensure direct alignment with specific standards, and inject fresh perspectives into your assessments while saving valuable time. The questions AI generates can serve as ready-to-use content or as starting points that you can modify to perfectly suit your learners' needs.

Here's how to get started crafting a quiz with AI:

1. First, tell the GPT what content you need to generate questions from. There are several options:
   - Copy and paste a text you wish to use into your GPT tool.
   - Upload a PDF or link to a file.

- Copy the link to content like a video, audio, or image file.
- In the Copilot sidebar in the Microsoft Edge browser or in a Chrome extension like Brisk, just open the website, then open the GPT tool on the side.
2. Write a prompt that gives the tool context about what you need. Include the age of your learners, how many questions you want, what type of questions you need, and if you want an answer key or not.

> **SAMPLE PROMPT**
>
> I am teaching ten-year-old learners about reptiles from around the world. We will read this article together. Write five questions I can use to assess their comprehension. The questions should be short-answer questions learners can answer in just a quick sentence. Provide an answer key.

I used this prompt with a web page about Burmese pythons from *National Geographic Kids*, and this is what generated:

> Certainly! Here are five comprehension questions with an answer key for your learners:
>
> Dietary habits: What do Burmese pythons eat?
>
> Answer: Small mammals, birds, and sometimes larger animals like pigs, goats, or alligators.
>
> Hunting method: How do Burmese pythons catch their prey?
>
> Answer: They use sharp teeth to seize prey and coil their body around it, squeezing tighter with each exhale until it suffocates.
>
> Physical growth: Where do young Burmese pythons spend their time and why do they change this behavior as they grow?
>
> Answer: They spend equal time on the ground and in trees when young but stay on the ground as they grow larger because trees can't hold them anymore.

Reproduction: How do female Burmese pythons care for their eggs?

<u>Answer: They lay clutches of up to one hundred eggs and incubate them by shivering their muscles to keep them warm.</u>

Survival skills: What do newly hatched baby pythons do after they hatch?

<u>Answer: They remain inside the egg until they finish shedding their first skin, then hunt for their first meal by themselves.</u>

Keep in mind you can follow this process with any content. Create questions from any of the following:

- YouTube video
- Audio file
- PDF
- Image
- Website

You don't have to resort to quiz questions either. You can ask for discussion prompts too! Here is a prompt I wrote for a TED-Ed video called "What Makes a Poem . . . a Poem?" by Melissa Kovacs. I used the Copilot sidebar in the Edge browser, so I just had the video open at the time. You can also drop the video URL into a web-connected app or export the video transcript to another GPT-style platform.

> **SAMPLE PROMPT**
>
> Use the transcript of this video to help me create some engaging discussion questions for a video that my learners will be watching. I'd like to encourage critical thinking and in-depth discussion among the learners. They are fifteen years old.

Here's what I got back:

Certainly! Here are some engaging discussion questions based on the video transcript that can encourage critical thinking and in-depth discussion among your fifteen-year-old learners:

[00:00:39]1 What is Poetry?

How do Muhammad Ali's words "Me, we" challenge the traditional definition of a poem?

Can two words constitute a poem, and why might this be considered the shortest poem ever?

[00:01:01]2 Musical Qualities of Language

In what ways do rhyme, rhythm, and meter contribute to the musicality of poetry?

Discuss examples of how different cultures use these elements in their poetic traditions.

[00:01:13]3 Condensed Language

Why is it important for poems to use condensed language, and how does it enhance the reader's experience?

Compare and contrast the impact of condensed language in poetry versus prose.

[00:01:23]4 Intense Feelings in Poetry

How do poets like Rumi and Pablo Neruda express intense feelings in their work?

What role do emotions play in the creation and interpretation of poetry?

[00:02:07]5 Poetry vs. Music

Are song lyrics considered poetry, and can they stand alone without music?

Debate the poetic elements in rap lyrics, using the example from the Notorious B.I.G. provided in the video.

[00:03:05]6 Prose Poems

> What are prose poems, and how do they differ from traditional poetry?
>
> Explore the concept of poetry beyond its form—can speeches, social media, and other forms of communication be poetic?

These questions are designed to spark a deeper understanding of poetry and its various forms, encouraging learners to think critically about language, culture, and expression—all while saving teachers time. That's the substitution level at its best. And when learners need more practice in a particular area but teachers are running low on energy, GPT, an AI app, or even Google Forms or Microsoft Forms (with AI) can be of particular value for generating question sets.

Brisk has a Chrome browser extension that easily creates Google Forms from content as well. What's lovely about a browser extension is that you don't have to leave the website you're viewing. I made a Google Forms quiz using Brisk's extension in approximately five clicks of my mouse. That's fast!

As another example, Microsoft's Math Progress allows teachers to generate a set of math questions based on a sample, then learners complete the questions. There is a lot more to Math Progress, but at this level, it's just a substitution for a teacher creating math problems.

Generative AI quiz creation saves educators valuable time while providing fresh perspectives and question types that may not have occurred to them. This simple substitution allows teachers to redirect their energy toward more complex instructional tasks while maintaining full editorial control over assessment content.

Create Student Surveys

Another great use for AI at the substitution level is creating surveys for learners to respond to, whether they're about a unit of study or a simple getting-to-know-you. I asked Copilot inside Microsoft Forms to create a survey for learners to take either before or on the first day of school.

> **SAMPLE PROMPT**
>
> Draft a getting-to-know-you form for twelve-year-old learners to let their teacher know a little about them before the start of the school year.

I was really happy with the results! The generative AI thought of some questions I hadn't, like asking learners how comfortable they were with public speaking, how they like to get help, and what activities they enjoy doing at school. It also created a variety of question types, which I thought was nice: ratings, drop-down menus, text responses, and multiple choice. I can edit these questions, of course, and regenerate questions if I'd like some other ideas. Just the time saved by not having to type these questions is worth it to me.

AI-powered survey generation offers educators a quick starting point for gathering student feedback without the time investment of creating questions from scratch. This straightforward substitution preserves the purpose and function of traditional surveys while reducing preparation time and potentially introducing question formats teachers might not have considered.

Generate Discussion Responses

Shout-out to the teacher on social media who I recently saw complaining that her learners were using generative AI to write replies for the weekly discussion prompts in their learning management system (LMS)! This seems like a great example of substitution. If we require learners to post their thinking and respond to each other, they might be using generative AI to create their posts and their replies. To do this well (and still meet the requirements for scoring), they have to write a solid prompt and include the content from the other learners. They may choose to copy and paste the output from generative AI, but if it meets the assignment criteria . . . either accept the work or create higher-level criteria!

Maybe the learners have the option of using generative AI to create their replies but must source it as a direct quote using APA or MLA format. Maybe the learners are required to include the output from generative AI as well as their evaluation of it. Maybe the learners are asked to use generative AI to craft their responses but are expected to evaluate them for accuracy, authenticity, and voice before posting them. There are many options here. Consider that learners who are already not invested in the discussions will write low-level responses just to meet the criteria. You may even have better results allowing learners to use GPTs to craft their replies!

> **SAMPLE PROMPT**
>
> I am a ninth-grade student in a world history class. My teacher created a discussion board where I have to post about one current world event that connects to an event in the history of the world. Write a short comparison statement for me to post for this assignment.

When I tried this sample prompt, the vocabulary for the response was much too high. I asked the tool to rewrite the reply "as a high school student with limited vocabulary," and I got the post shown below, which sounds a lot like a high school student. It also made a solid connection between the fighting in Gaza in 2024 and the Battle of Gettysburg in the American Civil War.

> Sure, here's a simpler version:
>
> "Right now, there's a big problem where Israel bombed a school in Gaza, and lots of people who weren't fighting got hurt. This is kind of like what happened a long time ago in the Battle of Gettysburg during the American Civil War. Back then, many people who weren't soldiers also got hurt, and it made people talk a lot about how wars should be fought and how to keep regular folks safe. The Battle of Gettysburg was a really important fight that changed the future of America. The things happening in Gaza today are also making people think about the rules of war and how to treat people fairly. It shows us that

> even though wars happen a long time apart, some things don't change, and we should try to learn from history so we don't have these sad things happen again."

Let's see what happens when generative AI writes a response to this post.

SAMPLE PROMPT

> I am a ninth-grade student in a world history class. My teacher created a discussion board where we all have to post about one current world event that connects to an event in the history of the world. I have to reply to my classmates with comments about their posts. One classmate wrote: "[paste response here]." Write a reply that I can use to comment on the post with an opinion. Use high school vocabulary.

The response not only gives the student an answer but also guides thinking. I really like how generative AI provided some guidance to how to respond, use empathy, and craft a reply.

> Your classmate has drawn a thoughtful parallel between the tragic events in Gaza and the historical Battle of Gettysburg. It's important to recognize that while wars may occur centuries apart, the human cost and the ethical considerations remain constant. The civilian suffering in both instances highlights the need for international laws and conventions that protect non-combatants during conflicts.
>
> In your response, you might consider acknowledging the gravity of the situation in Gaza and expressing hope that lessons from history can lead to a more peaceful future. You could also reflect on the role of global awareness and education in preventing such tragedies. Here's an example of how you might structure your comment:

> "Your comparison between the current events in Gaza and the Battle of Gettysburg is poignant. It's a stark reminder that despite advancements in warfare, the protection of civilians remains a critical issue. The international community must continue to strive for peace and uphold humanitarian principles to prevent such needless loss of life. As we learn from history, it's our collective responsibility to advocate for change and ensure that the horrors of war do not repeat themselves."
>
> Remember to use respectful language and express your thoughts in a way that contributes constructively to the discussion.

So many learners around the world do not have access to home support who could guide them this way. While this might seem like cheating, remember that the learners who *choose to learn* from this type of support will benefit greatly from the scaffolding and guidance. Learners who *choose to copy and paste* without digesting the content likely wouldn't have spent much time thinking about this type of assignment in the first place.

Draft Communications

Another great way to outsource work to generative AI is to ask for a draft of something you need to write: an email, family letter, or monthly newsletter. Format these prompts to include the audience, communication type, style, length, and purpose or topic. Once you have a prompt that works well for you, save it to reuse for future communications.

Prompt template:

> Write a [form] for [audience] that uses a [style] tone for [purpose or topic]. It should be [length in words or sentences] long.

> **SAMPLE PROMPT**
>
> Write an email for my students' families that uses a cheerful tone to inform them about our class butterfly station. Learners will be observing the life cycle of the butterfly all month long. This should be about ten sentences long.

Again, if you have a prompt that works for you, reuse it for a new purpose anytime.

> **SAMPLE PROMPT**
>
> Write an introduction to my third-grade class newsletter that uses a cheerful tone to inform them about our upcoming math unit on fractions. Learners will be focusing on identifying, adding, and subtracting fractions. Include a reference to how fractions can be observed in everyday life. This should be about two paragraphs long.

These types of communications are easy for generative AI to write in seconds. The work doesn't always end here, however. I often find that I edit generative AI-created text to fit my personal tone, but it still takes me less time to edit an output than it would to write from scratch. As an aside, when I do write from scratch, I tend to leave out enthusiastic remarks and friendly greetings. Generative AI often infuses a friendly tone (unless told not to, of course) because it is designed to be positive and kind. This writing style generally works well in student and family communications. For example, I have a write a newsletter for work, and I got tired of writing the introduction. I finally started asking AI to write it, and I got *positive feedback* from the audience that the newsletters were bright and cheerful. I'd never received that feedback when I wrote the intro by myself!

Remember, you can always remove or revise what generative AI writes. Having a good starting point is sometimes the largest battle in drafting great communications. At the very least, have AI generate an outline for you to start with. Speaking of outlines . . .

Written Work

Now we've come to one of the hottest and most controversial topics regarding AI in schools: learners using generative AI to support their written work. It's the literary version of the calculator doing the work for us while still requiring us to know how to use it properly to get the right results. Let's take that comparison a little further, since many of us in education are familiar with the use of calculators in school.

Consider that learners are only introduced to calculators after they have mastered some concepts of foundational numeracy. They begin using basic functions on calculators and are taught specifically how to use them. They learn what the different buttons do and how to get the right answer. Older learners receive access to more complex calculators and use them to check their work on computations or do the work entirely, in many cases. Once learners have mastered long division, for example, they are no longer required to perform it regularly. They use their calculators to save time and energy for more difficult tasks. In higher-level math, learners are trained in very complex calculators. In seconds, these devices perform functions that would take hours to do by hand. The calculator supports critical thinking, and learners only reach the correct answer by using the functions correctly. Teachers give instructions on how to input formulas into the specific calculator the learners have (or an online version, free through many apps now). On some standardized assessments, calculators are granted in one part and not in another. Teachers may ask learners not to use calculators for certain tests but allow them (or require them) in others. Some learners program cheats into their calculators so they don't have to memorize formulas, and they hope not to get caught.

Do you see the parallels? Within days of the arrival of ChatGPT's model for public use, I and many others started making this comparison. It took decades for education to embrace the calculator, and now everyone in the world with a mobile device carries a calculator in their pocket. They also now carry the power of generative AI in their pocket. Educators will need to approach generative AI in the same way.

In general, young students still need to learn how to print, type, form sentences, and use words properly. I believe they can be introduced to safe, closed systems of generative AI once they have the skills to interact with the tools. Following our calculator trajectory, older learners will learn how to use generative AI to complete tasks, how to prompt the tool, and how to check the outputs. As they get older, they will have access to more powerful GPTs and start to use them regularly to replace common tasks. Upper-level learners will use GPTs to do work that would have taken hours or days in seconds, allowing them to move on to higher thinking skills and bigger problems. If this prediction is true, what are appropriate ways for learners to use generative AI at a substitution level for the writing process?

The first way is for ideation. Generative AI does a great job of hurdling writer's block! It's a creative tool for the stuck writer. It generates suggestions, ideas, and lists, and it brainstorms with ease. Think about the time you may have spent as an educator (or home support!) in getting a student started. You coach and coax through each beginning step just to get an idea going, and then the student can begin writing. GPTs are great at this task, and they are available for everyone, everywhere. Teachers multiply their efforts from one-to-one to one-to-many support, and all learners, regardless of home situation, can get this support. It is a substitution for a human, but a powerful one.

> **SAMPLE PROMPT**
>
> I am a thirteen-year-old student writing a story for an assignment at school. My story has to include a hero, a villain, and a journey. I'd like to use story elements that I enjoy like skateboarding and pizza. Help me come up with ideas for the basic plot of my story.

When I tried this prompt in four different GPTs, each one returned a basic overview of a story, including suggestions for a title, a hero, supporting characters, a villain, a journey, conflict or obstacles, and a resolution. Some even included themes, like friendship or empathy. One interesting point I will make here is about the character names. Copilot and ChatGPT, both trained on the OpenAI model, returned the same name for the main character. The letter x was prevalent in the names used in three of the tools. Most of the names were short and common. In fact, I tried the same prompt a few times, and Max was the hero every time! Latimer, which is designed to bring out "diverse histories and inclusive voices," used a completely different style for the names.

GPT Tool	Copilot	ChatGPT	Poe	Latimer
Hero and sidekick names	Max	Max, Sam, Maria, and Dex	Zoe and Alex	Jamal
Villian name	Razer	Tony	Mr. Slimeball	Tyrone

This is a consideration when working with generative AI as we think about representation for our learners and bringing in new perspectives.

The next way learners could use generative AI in the writing process is outlining. This too has been around for years. Microsoft PowerPoint has had QuickStarter for about a decade! QuickStarter generates a set of slides and an outline to research based on your topic of choice, and it can even add images and text to the slides as suggestions. It's an AI-powered support that gives a framework for whatever topic you choose. Generative AI can create an outline for a presentation, a research paper, a narrative, or a design project. In this case learners are substituting their own work for a scaffolded template of sorts—a starting point. They can edit the outline, of course, and make changes based on their focus or the assignment directions. But it's incredibly powerful to have a starting point. Learners who struggle with executive function are most supported by these types of output. Breaking big topics into small pieces is a complex task, and teachers spend precious minutes modeling this for learners in whole-group settings before unleashing them to practice on their own, not to mention coaching students who get stuck. GPTs can enhance efficiency by providing an outline and giving learners a starting point.

> **SAMPLE PROMPT**
>
> Act like a high school student writing an essay about the reasons countries have civil wars. The essay needs to include different examples from countries around the world over the last few hundred years. Create an outline for the essay that I can use to begin research.

All the apps I tried with this prompt returned an outline that included political, social, economic, and cultural factors. Most returned a similar set of examples, from the American Civil War to civil wars in Syria, Lebanon, Rwanda, and Yugoslavia. Two models returned research tips at the end as well. I appreciate that some models' responses encouraged fact-checking with primary sources!

What about drafting? Now we're getting into especially controversial territory! What if learners used generative AI to create a draft for their writing? In a classroom scenario, teachers might guide learners to ideate with AI, then create an outline (and revise that outline), and then ask a GPT to create a draft based on that outline. This is an iterative process. Learners receive a draft they would have spent time writing on their own (hence the substitution level), and they instead spend time revising, editing, and refining the draft before it becomes their own work.

A parallel to this is common in education. Consider the research project. Learners read books or websites, take notes, and write their own work. The whole time, they are reading someone else's words and refining them into their own. They take content they did not write and refine it by analyzing, summarizing, evaluating, and synthesizing. With generative AI, learners are provided with one more piece of text. It's uniquely generated just for them, based on their prompt instead of based on several internet searches. If they use this text as a jumping-off point, they are skipping the step of synthesizing the searches themselves. But they should also be responsible for fact-checking the sources and confirming their information is sound.

One of my favorite ways for learners to use drafting to their advantage is to give the GPT a sample of their own writing and then ask for multiple options. They are then expected to choose the best language from the responses and synthesize them into one final work.

> **SAMPLE PROMPT**
>
> Learn my writing style. Next write a conclusion statement for my persuasive speech on the importance of good sleep. [Copy and paste the written portion of the essay here.] Edit the content to match my style and vocabulary level. Then provide two more options as alternative endings.

Allowing learners to use generative AI to support writing projects beyond this point falls into the other levels of SAMR, so we'll save that for another chapter. Meanwhile, I encourage you to challenge your thinking around generative AI in the writing process. I am a firm believer that it has a proper place.

AUGMENTATION

Content Generation

Content generation with AI goes beyond simply producing worksheets; it's about creating dynamic, relevant materials that support and enhance what's happening in the classroom. In traditional teaching, educators spend significant time developing lesson plans, creating worksheets, and finding resources that align with their curriculum. AI-powered content-generation tools augment this process by providing functional improvements that make it more efficient and effective. AI can help educators generate a variety of educational resources (say it with me: not just another worksheet) tailored to the specific needs and interests of their learners.

One creative use of AI in content generation is in developing real-world problem-solving scenarios. Suppose you're teaching a math class. Instead of traditional problem sets, you can use AI to create scenarios that require learners to apply mathematical concepts to solve real-world problems such as budgeting for a school event or analyzing data from a science experiment that was conducted by the students. These scenarios can be adjusted based on the learners' interests and the current topics being covered in class, making the learning experience more relevant and engaging. Hot tip from me to you: Use AI to generate math problems based on pop culture and your learners' high-interest topics.

> **SAMPLE PROMPT**
>
> Write a math problem for a pre-algebra class that uses data from Taylor Swift's Eras Tour.

Results:

> Taylor Swift's Eras Tour has been a massive success. During the US leg of her tour, she performed fifty-three shows, each attracting an average of seventy-two thousand spectators (statista.com). The average ticket price for these shows was $238 (rollingstone.com).
>
> Calculate the total number of spectators who attended the US leg of the tour.
>
> Determine the total revenue generated from ticket sales during the US leg of the tour.

AI can help generate personalized reading materials too. Ask a GPT to create a piece of text with your learners' names and details about your school or a topic of interest to students. Keep in mind that historical pieces should be accurate to the time period and should be respectful of the cultural references.

> **SAMPLE PROMPT 1**
>
> Write a historical fiction piece about two children, one from a traditional samurai family and the other from a merchant family. They experience the dramatic changes of the era. They witness the clash between old traditions and new ways of life, and their friendship helps them navigate these changes. There is a koi pond in their village. Use Lexile level 600. It should be about five hundred words long. Incorporate sweet treats, playing outside, and having to take a test.

> **SAMPLE PROMPT 2**
>
> Write a six-stanza poem in ABBA format that includes details about animal habitats. Include the names Anya and Toby, Millennium Elementary School, eagles, and Mrs. Keene.

Results from prompt 2:

In the heart of the forest, where the tall trees sway
Anya and Toby explore with glee
At Millennium Elementary, they learn and see
The wonders of nature, each and every day

Mrs. Keene guides them through the marsh so green
Where frogs leap and dragonflies dart
In the wetlands, they play their part
In the balance of life, so serene

To the desert they go, where the sun beats down
Cacti stand tall, and lizards scurry

> Anya and Toby, they never hurry
> Learning from Mrs. Keene, they wear no frown
>
> In the ocean deep, where the coral reefs glow
> Fish of all colors swim in schools
> At Millennium Elementary, they follow the rules
> Respecting the sea, where the currents flow
>
> Up in the mountains, where the eagles soar
> Anya and Toby hike with care
> Mrs. Keene teaches them to be aware
> Of the habitats that they adore
>
> In the Arctic cold, where the polar bears roam
> They learn of ice and snow so white
> At Millennium Elementary, they gain insight
> Into the world's vast, diverse biome

AI can also assist in creating multimedia presentations that incorporate videos, images, and interactive elements. For instance, if you're teaching a history lesson, an AI tool can help you compile a presentation that includes historical footage, interactive timelines, and primary source documents. This not only makes the lesson more engaging but also caters to different learning styles.

There are probably a million AI-powered presentation generators by now. At least, it feels like that many! Microsoft PowerPoint has been the gold standard in presentation software for a long time, but tools like Canva and Google Slides offer similar functionality. You probably already have access to at least one of those tools, if not all three. But there are many other presentation creators that are more interactive and allow for highly customized content, and most will export neatly into your favorite platform. A tool made for presentations should have certain codes and algorithms that will generate better results. Take a look at Beautiful.ai, PopAi, Gamma, and SlidesAI for a start. I suggest setting aside a couple of hours and trying to create a presentation on the same topic with multiple tools. It gives you a purpose, a pathway to find all the best features, and immediate comparison points.

Please don't focus on creating teacher-led presentations from other multimedia content like videos, though. Remember this from the first chapter of the book? It feels like a step in the wrong direction, without a *really* good purpose.

Creating a presentation for learners feels like substitution . . . until you add multimedia elements that you never would have created. It's the functional improvement of being able to ask for what you want. A powerful tool will pull together facts, data, layout, imagery, and format from just a prompt—and the output is gorgeous. That's certainly a benefit to the presenter and the audience.

> The most innovative educators aren't necessarily the most tech-savvy! They're the ones who maintain a learner's mindset. Approach AI with the same curiosity you hope to inspire in your students, and you'll discover capabilities you never knew you had.

MODIFICATION

Video Engagement

In part thanks to the year 2020, video meetings have become an integral part of modern education. We completely changed how we connect, collaborate, and learn across distances. From virtual classrooms and parent conferences to staff meetings and professional development sessions, educators now spend countless hours engaging through video platforms.

This shift has created both opportunities and challenges. While video enables connection regardless of location, many participants report feeling disengaged or fatigued during lengthy sessions. The standard video meeting format, with its grid of faces and limited interaction options, can feel static and impersonal compared to in-person gatherings.

Educators can leverage AI-generated avatars in video meetings to level up the teaching experience in several innovative ways. These avatars, powered by advanced AI algorithms, can create a more engaging, personalized, and inclusive learning environment.

For example, platforms like Synthesia allow educators to create AI avatars that can deliver lectures, answer questions, and provide feedback in real time. This can make virtual lessons (or even video-recorded flipped lessons) more dynamic and captivating, especially for younger learners who might find traditional videos less engaging. I've seen educators use characters to enhance a video lesson, adding a filter to appear as an animal, person in history, or famous celebrity.

More advanced AI avatars even offer personalized learning experiences. They can adapt their responses based on individual learners' needs and progress. For instance, an AI avatar can provide additional explanations or resources to a learner who is struggling with a particular concept, ensuring that each student receives the support they need to succeed.

AI avatars can facilitate inclusivity and accessibility in education. They can provide content in multiple languages, adapt to learning disabilities, and offer captions for learners with hearing impairments. This ensures that all learners, regardless of their abilities or backgrounds, have equal access to quality education.

Additionally, AI avatars can help in maintaining a consistent teaching presence. For example, if an educator is unavailable, an AI avatar can step in to deliver pre-recorded lessons or interact with learners, ensuring that the learning process is not disrupted. This can be particularly useful in large classes or in situations where one-on-one interaction is needed but not always feasible.

Another benefit of using AI avatars is they enhance collaborative learning. In virtual group projects, they can mediate discussions, suggest resources, and ensure that all learners are participating and contributing effectively. This can lead to more productive and balanced group work, creating a collaborative learning environment.

By integrating AI-generated avatars into video content, educators can make lessons more interactive, personalized, and inclusive. This is a redefinition of the traditional teaching experience.

Exemplars

I was talking to a secondary language arts teacher after an AI-centered professional development event I led at her school, and she commented that she always provided her students with exemplar texts during a writing assignment but that many times they asked for additional examples or more explanation of the example text. As we talked, she acknowledged that she could have her students create their own exemplar texts using generative AI. That way, they could get to know the prompt better, ask for explanations, and see samples of great writing.

The teacher I was working with got really excited about this idea. Then I recommended her students could even keep track of great prompts that worked for creating high-quality examples. They could learn from these, use them for essay help, and even share them in a collective prompt library. This teacher walked off smiling and planning to create a space for her students to use immediately.

What's to keep these learners from copying and pasting the exemplar text as their own essay? Nothing, really, outside of academic integrity. The teacher might use a tool like Brisk that allows her to check the student work history for copy/paste actions, but ultimately that's time-consuming. It's also hyperfocused on catching cheating, which is not how I'd ever recommend educators spend their time. Let's take a look at a prompt that could be useful for creating an exemplar and see how AI handles it.

> **SAMPLE PROMPT**
>
> I am a sophomore in an English writing class. My teacher gave us the following essay assignment. I want to write my own essay but I am stuck. I'd like some help. First, please provide step-by-step directions on how to brainstorm my own ideas for my essay. Then, draft a sample outline for an essay for this topic. Next, provide a sample essay for me to review. Finally, write some reflection questions to help me evaluate the sample essay, looking for key points and helping me understand how to write my own essay successfully.
>
> [Here is the prompt from the teacher.] In *O Beautiful*, Jung Yun explores complex themes such as identity, belonging, and the American dream. As you reflect on the book, consider how these themes are developed through the characters, plot, and setting.
>
> Write a reflective essay that examines how the theme of identity is portrayed in *O Beautiful*. In your essay, consider the following questions:
>
> Character analysis: How do the main characters in the book struggle with or embrace their identities? Provide specific examples from the text to support your analysis.
>
> Cultural context: How does the cultural and historical context of the story influence the characters' sense of identity? Discuss how the setting and time period impact their experiences and perspectives.
>
> Personal connection: Reflect on your own experiences or observations related to identity. How do the characters' journeys resonate with you or challenge your understanding of identity?

> Literary devices: Analyze how Jung Yun uses literary devices such as symbolism, imagery, and dialogue to convey the theme of identity. How do these elements enhance your understanding of the characters' struggles and growth?
>
> Guidelines:
>
> Your essay should be three to four pages long, double-spaced, with twelve-point Times New Roman font.
>
> Use specific quotes and examples from the book to support your analysis.
>
> Organize your essay with a clear introduction, body paragraphs, and a conclusion.
>
> Proofread your essay for grammar, spelling, and clarity before submitting.

I tried this prompt in Copilot (GPT-4 Turbo), ChatGPT (GPT-4o), Claude 3.7, and Perplexity. While the results between the models were similar, I thought Copilot did the best job of scaffolding. I did like the way Claude ended with a reminder to use the essay as a sample and then write a new one with the guiding questions. Learners would be served well by any of these options, or you could set up a space just for this purpose in a tool like SchoolAI.

Sample response:

> Step-by-Step Directions for Brainstorming Ideas
>
> Understand the prompt: Carefully read the essay prompt and guidelines. Identify the key themes and questions you need to address.
>
> Read and annotate: Revisit *O Beautiful* and take notes on passages that relate to identity. Highlight quotes and scenes that stand out.

Character analysis: List the main characters and jot down how each one struggles with or embraces their identity. Note specific examples from the text.

Cultural context: Reflect on the cultural and historical context of the story. How does the setting influence the characters' identities?

Personal connection: Think about your own experiences with identity. How do the characters' journeys resonate with you?

Literary devices: Identify literary devices Jung Yun uses to convey the theme of identity. Look for symbolism, imagery, and dialogue.

Organize your thoughts: Group your notes into categories that align with the essay questions. This will help you structure your essay.

Sample Outline for the Essay

Introduction

Hook: A compelling quote or question about identity

Brief overview of *O Beautiful* and its themes

Thesis statement: How the theme of identity is portrayed in the book

Body Paragraph 1: Character Analysis

Topic sentence: Main characters' struggles with identity

Example 1: Character A's journey

Example 2: Character B's journey

Analysis: How these examples illustrate the theme of identity

Body Paragraph 2: Cultural Context

Topic sentence: Influence of cultural and historical context

Example 1: Setting's impact on Character A

Example 2: Time period's impact on Character B

Analysis: How the context shapes their identities

Body paragraph 3: Personal Connection

Topic sentence: Personal reflections on identity

Example 1: Your own experience related to Character A

Example 2: Observations related to Character B

Analysis: How these connections deepen your understanding of identity

Body Paragraph 4: Literary Devices

Topic sentence: Use of literary devices to convey identity

Example 1: Symbolism in the book

Example 2: Imagery and dialogue

Analysis: How these devices enhance the theme of identity

Conclusion

Restate thesis in light of the analysis

Summarize key points

Closing thought: Reflect on the broader implications of identity in the book and in real life

Sample Essay

Title: Exploring Identity in Jung Yun's *O Beautiful*

Introduction: Identity is a multifaceted concept that shapes our experiences and perceptions. In Jung Yun's novel *O Beautiful*, the theme of identity is intricately woven through the characters, plot, and setting. This essay explores how the main characters grapple with their identities, the influence of cultural and historical contexts, personal connections to the theme, and the literary devices used to convey these struggles.

Character Analysis: The main characters in *O Beautiful* each face unique challenges related to their identities. Character A, for instance, struggles with reconciling their cultural heritage with their desire to fit into mainstream society. This internal conflict is evident in scenes where Character A feels torn between family expectations and personal aspirations. Similarly, Character B embraces their identity more openly, using their experiences to advocate for social change. These characters' journeys highlight the complexities of identity and the different ways individuals navigate their sense of self.

Cultural Context: The cultural and historical context of *O Beautiful* plays a significant role in shaping the characters' identities. Set in a time of social upheaval, the story reflects the tensions and opportunities of the era. Character A's experiences are deeply influenced by the cultural expectations of their community, while Character B's actions are shaped by the broader historical movements of the time. The setting and time period provide a backdrop that amplifies the characters' struggles and growth.

Personal Connection: Reflecting on my own experiences, I find parallels between the characters' journeys and my understanding of identity. Like Character A, I have felt the pressure to conform to societal norms while trying to honor my cultural background. Observing Character B's resilience and advocacy inspires me to embrace my identity more fully. These personal connections make the theme of identity in *O Beautiful* resonate on a deeper level.

Literary Devices: Jung Yun employs various literary devices to enhance the theme of identity. Symbolism is used effectively, with certain objects and settings representing the characters' internal conflicts. Imagery and dialogue further convey the emotional depth of their struggles. For example, the recurring motif of a broken mirror symbolizes the fragmented nature of identity, while the characters' conversations reveal their innermost fears and hopes. These devices enrich the narrative and provide a deeper understanding of the characters' journeys.

Conclusion: In *O Beautiful*, Jung Yun masterfully explores the theme of identity through complex characters, a rich cultural context, and powerful literary devices. The characters' struggles and growth offer valuable insights into the multifaceted nature of identity. As readers, we are invited to reflect on our own experiences and consider the broader implications of identity in our lives.

Reflection Questions

Character analysis: How effectively does the essay analyze the main characters' struggles with identity? Are the examples from the text specific and relevant?

Cultural context: Does the essay clearly explain how the cultural and historical context influences the characters' identities? Are the connections to the setting and time period well developed?

Personal connection: How well does the essay integrate personal reflections on identity? Do these reflections enhance the overall analysis?

Literary devices: How effectively does the essay analyze the use of literary devices to convey the theme of identity? Are the examples of symbolism, imagery, and dialogue clear and insightful?

Organization and clarity: Is the essay well-organized with a clear introduction, body paragraphs, and conclusion? Are the ideas presented logically and coherently?

Proofreading: Are there any grammatical, spelling, or clarity issues that need to be addressed? How can the essay be improved in terms of language and style?

I hope this helps you get started on your essay! Feel free to ask if you need further assistance.

Enabling learners to create their own worked examples can give guidance where they would normally falter on their own. Prompts like these allow learners to use generative AI to create examples and walk through the thinking involved. This is a completely new task. It's not about checking student work after it's done—it's about creating a sample ahead of the work.

AI-generated worked examples give students on-demand access to personalized step-by-step guidance that adjusts to their specific questions and learning needs. This modification of traditional example problems creates a more responsive learning experience where students receive immediate support while maintaining agency over their learning process.

CONCLUSION

Artificial intelligence offers massive potential for how teachers, students, and administrators create educational content. By applying the SAMR framework, we can progress from using AI to overcome common constraints to reimagining what's possible in educational creation.

For teachers, AI transitions content creation from a sometimes overwhelming necessity into an opportunity for enhanced creativity and personalization. No longer limited to generic worksheets or recycled materials, educators can now generate customized resources aligned with their unique teaching style and their students' specific needs, even under tight time constraints. The routine aspects of creation become efficient, leaving more energy for the creative elements that make learning memorable.

For students, AI tools provide scaffolding that helps them break out of formulaic approaches. Rather than produce predictable essays or presentations, learners can use AI to explore different styles, receive immediate feedback, and develop work that truly reflects their understanding and creative thinking. This support empowers students to take greater ownership of their work, building confidence along with skills.

For administrators and school leaders, AI enables the creation of communications and resources that stand out rather than blend in. Messages can be tailored to specific audiences, data can be presented in compelling visual formats, and routine documents can be generated quickly, allowing more time for the strategic thinking and relationship building that truly matter.

Perhaps most importantly, AI-supported content creation changes the experience of creating itself. When the burden of routine generation is lifted, everyone in the educational ecosystem can approach creation with renewed enthusiasm and innovation. Teachers can experiment with fresh approaches, students can express themselves more authentically, and administrators can communicate more effectively. Everyone can begin to feel more empowered in their respective roles.

As you implement these content-creation approaches in your own context, remember that AI serves as a collaborative partner that amplifies your creativity rather than replaces it. The most powerful applications come when human expertise, empathy, and wisdom are enhanced by AI's capabilities, allowing everyone in the educational ecosystem to create materials that inspire, engage, and drive innovation.

In the next chapter, we'll move from creation to support, exploring how AI can help implement and sustain effective learning experiences. While creation provides the content, support ensures that every learner has what they need to succeed.

7

SUPPORT

THE BELL RINGS, AND THERE are thirty students in my seventh-grade classroom. Among them is Student 1, who arrived from an island in Micronesia three months ago and is still developing his English-language skills. There's also Student 2, who reads three grade levels above her peers and quickly grows bored with standard assignments. She has volleyball tryouts today, and she's distracted. In the back row sits Student 3, who struggles with dyslexia and finds text-heavy lessons overwhelming. Nearby him is Student 4, who excels verbally but freezes during written assessments—and never gets to eat breakfast.

A single classroom containing wildly different learning needs, abilities, and backgrounds, is the daily reality for educators everywhere. The traditional one-size-fits-all approach to education has never truly fit all, but until recently, the practical limitations of providing personalized support to every student seemed insurmountable. Even the most dedicated teachers, working with the best intentions, face significant constraints of time, resources, and attention when trying to differentiate instruction for twenty-five to thirty-five students simultaneously.

Supporting diverse learners has always been education's greatest challenge and most important mission. Research consistently confirms what educators already know: Students learn best when instruction and resources align with their individual needs, interests, and learning preferences. When properly supported, every student can achieve success. Providing that personalized support traditionally requires more time and resources than most settings can realistically offer.

The promise of AI-powered support is not just efficiency but equity. Students who have historically had less access to individualized attention—whether due to large class sizes, limited resources, or systemic barriers—stand to gain the most from well-implemented AI support systems. However, this requires intentional design that considers the needs of students with varied linguistic backgrounds, learning differences, and cultural contexts.

This is where artificial intelligence is a changemaker. Unlike previous educational technologies that often provided the same experience to all users, AI has the unique capability to adapt, personalize, and respond to individual needs at scale. It can provide immediate, tailored feedback when a student struggles with a concept, offer appropriate challenges to those who have mastered the basics, and present information in multiple formats to accommodate different learning preferences simultaneously, without exhausting human resources.

Through the SAMR framework, we can see how AI progressively shifts the way we support learners:

At the *substitution* level, AI can provide basic literacy support, answer frequently asked questions, assist with information searches, and check math solutions.

Moving to *augmentation*, AI enhances support through learner chatbots, personalized learning platforms, and virtual

> Perhaps nowhere is AI optimism more apparent for me than in our ability as educators to finally provide the personalized support that we know is impactful. AI creates space for human connections by handling the aspects of support that can be systematized, allowing educators to focus on the aspects that cannot.

coaching sessions that provide more tailored and responsive assistance than traditional methods could offer.

At the *modification* level, AI fundamentally changes how support is provided, enabling truly personalized college and career guidance, competency-based skill building, mental health support, and more.

This chapter explores practical ways that teachers, students, and administrators can implement AI-powered support systems. Rather than replace the essential human relationships at the heart of education, these tools expand our capacity to meet each learner where they are. It's about providing the right support, at the right time, in the right format.

SUBSTITUTION

AI-Powered Literacy Support

Many learners benefit from translation tools, accessibility features, dictation, and narration. While not generative, AI supports for literacy have also been available for years. Dictation substitutes for the student typing or writing every thought. Research tells us many learners will capture more thoughts if they can dictate because spelling and typing skills don't get in the way of ideation. They can also benefit from speaking their thoughts first, then editing them later. Learners might also need to hear their writing read aloud to check for errors. Read-aloud tools give learners a chance to build comprehension through audio input in addition to visual input. And translation, of course, means people everywhere can interact with text in their preferred language.

My very favorite tool for translation is my iPhone camera. I can snap a photo of a sign or placard anywhere and use the Photos app to select the text and translate on-screen. You don't need generative AI to translate text. You just need an internet connection and a translation service. In education, my favorite tool for translation is Immersive Reader. It's available in all sorts of apps, including the core Microsoft apps as well as Pear Deck, Nearpod, Wakelet, Flocabulary, Buncee,

Canvas, Schoology, Skooler, and more. Read Aloud inside Immersive Reader is a substitution for another human reading the text aloud to a student who couldn't otherwise be successful. They don't need to wait for a turn, raise their hand, or ask for help.

AI-powered literacy tools substitute for traditional reading supports by offering translation, dictation, and text-to-speech capabilities without human intervention. These accessible features allow students to engage with content more independently while removing barriers that might otherwise limit their access to information.

Frequently Asked Questions

If you're working in any sort of technical support role, you are likely making mental notes of the questions you get asked. You might then create support documentation around the hot topics you've noticed. I've talked to some instructional coaches who literally keep sticky notes around the office and make a tally mark every time they get asked about a topic. Once the tally reaches ten, they make a support document or video snip to reduce further questions.

With an enterprise tool, you can ask for this tally without doing it yourself. This prompt is easy. Just ask something like this:

> **SAMPLE PROMPT**
>
> Make a list of the top ten questions I've been asked about [technology or topic] in the past year.

When I was leading professional development for my district's one-to-one device initiative, I found myself constantly answering the same questions about basic troubleshooting. After creating a simple FAQ, I shared it with teachers at the start of each training session via our district website. The number of interruptions dropped dramatically, and our sessions became much more focused on pedagogical applications rather than technical issues. What took me hours to compile years ago could have been generated in minutes with AI, saving everyone valuable time and improving the quality of our professional learning.

AI-generated FAQ documents efficiently substitute for the time-consuming process of manually tracking and answering repetitive questions, allowing educators and support staff to focus on more complex issues that require human expertise. The time saved can be redirected toward deeper support that makes a difference for students and colleagues.

Information Searches (Research)

I spent the early 2000s teaching learners and adults how to conduct web searches to find information. Web searching is a concrete skill. Searchers have to phrase questions a certain way to optimize results. Search results have been skewed over time by search engine optimization (SEO) and paid advertising, among other algorithms that present information to us based on the preference of the search engine's coding. It can take several searches to find the right information, and most people never click past the first page of search results. Top hits are managed by paid advertisers, and sometimes learners cite "Google" as their source of information because they never even opened the website itself. Problems abound.

Tools like Microsoft's Search Coach can help learners understand many of these issues, including how to search the internet for domains and filters, how to evaluate for bias and write neutral searches, etc. This is a good step in AI literacy. Another step is to teach learners how to evaluate the results of a generative AI output.

Learners often say searching for information with generative AI feels natural. Many of our young people have grown up using voice-activated assistants like Siri and Alexa. Adults have modeled talking to these assistants with their requests to play a song, turn out the lights, get directions. Conversational prompting shows that learners have no problem bossing around their digital assistants! This natural language processing power becomes amplified inside a GPT.

With AI, instead of learning how to use a search engine, learners ask questions conversationally. They type or dictate exactly what they're thinking, as if they're talking to another person. And the results sound like they're coming from another person! This makes generative AI prompting more accessible for learners since it's only relying on their conversational language skills. Evaluating the results, however, is a skill that still needs our attention. Consider Wikipedia. When this crowdsourced information hub first appeared, the education system had serious concerns about its use. Over time, Wikipedia proved that the editors, grading and feedback system, and community standards it had in place could correct erroneous information quickly. Many teachers taught learners to use Wikipedia *as a starting point* for research. The source links and footnotes on the page, along with the article itself, gave learners an overview of information plus the opportunity to follow the links and learn more. This is exactly how generative AI should be used for research. Information search is a substitution because this information is available on the internet. A student could spend hours searching, reading, clicking, and scrolling. Or they could ask generative AI to consolidate billions of data points into one output and read that. It's hard to argue with the efficiency. AI tools such as Elicit, Humata, Scite, Consensus, and Genei can find relevant papers, summarize them, and answer questions. Recently many platforms have released a model in the style of Think Deeper, which considers more connections and uses more processing power to reason and generate more thoughtful outputs. You can even ask these apps to pose as the author of the paper and conduct an interview based on its contents. Interesting—and that's definitely beyond substitution.

Consider asking learners to use an app that includes source links for its information. Copilot and Perplexity include sources by default and always have. ChatGPT and Gemini updated to include links in your output, especially if you ask for them. Claude announced web results in March 2025. It seems the feature is worth having!

Keep in mind the age of the original data set for whatever tool you use. Apps that use web grounding can return results from the live internet, so its results will always be current, but they are still trained with a data set that stopped at some point. Whatever tool you use, it's important that students learn to check the sources for reliability, accuracy, bias, relevance, and date. Teach learners to read laterally (to follow links to more information) so they have a full picture of the data being used to generate output.

Learners can also ask for a list of websites directly. If learners were looking for a new book to read and didn't know where to begin, they might ask generative AI to give them an idea of where to start. I asked several different apps the same prompt: Give me five websites that talk book reviews. Here's what I got back.

Copilot	ChatGPT	Claude	Latimer	Perplexity	Poe
Goodreads	BookBrowse	Goodreads	Goodreads	Goodreads	Goodreads
LibraryThing	Reedsy Discovery	The New York Times Book Review	The Root	LibraryThing	The New York Times Book Review
The Millions	Book Marks	BookPage	Electric Literature	BookBub	NPR Books
NetGalley	The Millions	Kirkus Reviews	Oprah's Book Club	Kirkus Reviews	Kirkus Reviews
Book Riot	BookTrib	The Guardian Books	Essence	The New York Times Book Review	Book Riot

I include this chart because my analytical brain can't help but wonder why ChatGPT left out the top website returned by every other app! I also want to point out Latimer's response, which stated in the output that the results "include those that specifically focus on books by Black authors or with themes related to Black culture and history." While there is no correct answer for a list of five book review websites, we can see trends in responses and use this to inform our decisions about which apps to use for our purposes. All six apps returned clickable links to the websites.

I love that Perplexity's suggested follow-up question to this output was "How does Goodreads compare to LibraryThing in terms of user experience?" It's great to get kids thinking about what to ask next. Follow-up questions enhance the search experience because they prompt humans to dig deeper. This gives learners the opportunity to see what they might have been missing and learn a little more. It's the learning equivalent of the entertainment-focused AI that presents us with "you also might enjoy" and shows us another song, movie, or game. It's the substitution for a textbook pop-out box that begins with "Did you know?" Teach learners to check the suggested follow-up questions if the app they're using includes them.

Math Solution Checker

When it comes to mathematical problem-solving, AI has been doing a great job for years. Tools like Photomath and WolframAlpha use a device camera to capture the problem on paper or in a textbook, then provide a solution as well as the answer steps. It's the digital equivalent of checking the answers to the odd problems in the back of the book. It's substitution if the student only checks for the right answer, which many of them do. But it allows learners to check all their work, and all of their answers, not just the odd problems, and not just the ones that a home support human can figure out.

This functionality might be especially interesting to math and science teachers (specifically physics or chemistry). When we teach learners how valuable these tools can be, some of them will choose to learn from them. The other learners will use them for quick answers, and you can't do anything about that. But you can remember that the primacy effect matters when learning new skills—learners who misunderstand and then practice a misstep in math or science are most likely to repeat it, over and over. It often takes until after an assessment for a learner to correct a misconception, and by then it might be too late.

Example: Learner uses a math solver app to take a photo of the problem on a worksheet or in a textbook.

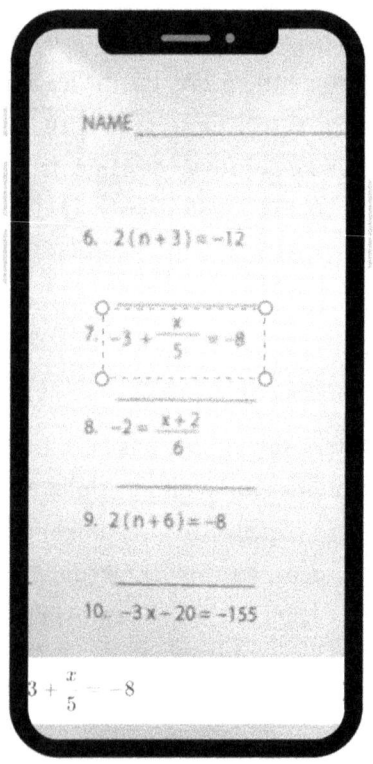 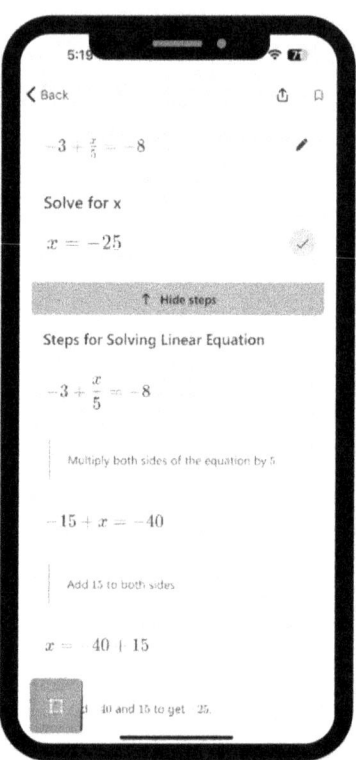

At the bottom of the response screen, learners are prompted to try more examples similar to the problem solved and take a self-assessment quiz with the same type of questions.

Students could also prompt generative AI to help them with this style of problem.

SUPPORT | 109

SAMPLE PROMPT

I have a math problem to solve. I'm not sure where to start, but I don't want you to give me the answer. Walk me through the steps of solving a similar math problem first. Then ask me one question at a time to help me solve the problem in my book. Wait for me to respond after each question. Correct my work as we go along.

Here's what that response looks like in ChatGPT:

Let's start by walking through a similar problem so you can get comfortable with the steps.

Similar Problem:

Suppose we have the equation $-4 = \frac{c}{8}$, and we want to solve for c.

Step 1: Identify the equation.

- The equation is $-4 = \frac{c}{8}$.

Step 2: Isolate the variable.

- To solve for c, we need to get c by itself on one side of the equation. We can do this by multiplying both sides of the equation by the denominator (in this case, 8) to cancel out the fraction.

So, multiply both sides by 8:

$$8 \times -4 = 8 \times \frac{c}{8}$$

Step 3: Simplify the equation.

- On the left side, multiply 8 by -4.

Now let's solve the problem in your book. Look at the problem from the image, which is $-3 = \frac{b}{12}$.

Question 1:

What do you think the first step should be to solve for b in this equation?

Multiply both sides by 12.

Great job! That's exactly the right first step.

Step 1: Multiply both sides of the equation by 12 to isolate b.

Starting with:

$$-3 = \frac{b}{12}$$

Multiply both sides by 12:

Any caregiver who remembers a child in tears over math homework will appreciate having these tools available. Teaching students to use them appropriately and productively gives every student a chance to come to school with a corrected assignment—saving valuable class and teacher time.

AUGMENTATION

Learner Chatbots

Learner-facing chatbots are emerging as a powerful tool to support both students and educators. These AI-driven virtual assistants can perform a variety of tasks, enhancing the educational experience by providing timely and personalized support. A student chatbot can answer common questions about school policies, schedules, and resources, offering instant assistance that reduces the burden on administrative and office staff. For instance, if a learner needs to know the date of the next exam or the procedure for submitting an assignment, the chatbot can provide immediate, accurate information. Even more beneficial is if learners can access these systems alongside their home support humans, from anywhere (especially via mobile).

The use cases for student chatbots are diverse and impactful. They can assist with homework by providing explanations and resources for various subjects, acting as a supplementary tutor available 24/7. Additionally, chatbots can facilitate communication between learners and teachers by relaying messages and reminders, ensuring that important information is not missed. In a more advanced capacity, chatbots can monitor student well-being by analyzing interactions and flagging potential issues, such as signs of stress or disengagement, allowing for timely interventions. These types of chatbots include wellness check-ins, polls, and surveys for anyone using the tool.

Chatbots offer a scalable solution to provide consistent support, ensuring that every learner has access to the help they need, regardless of the time of day. Many learners may actually prefer the automated, digital approach to asking questions. No chatbot is going to roll its eyes and sigh at having to answer the same question for the umpteenth time. This can be particularly beneficial in large schools where individual attention is more limited. Chatbots also free up valuable time for educators and administrative staff, allowing them to focus on more complex tasks that require human intervention. The data collected by chatbots can provide insights into student needs and behaviors, informing better decision-making and personalized learning strategies. Administrators can use the analytics from the chatbots to clarify learner- and community-facing content so more questions are answered ahead of time. This level of proactive solution can reduce frustration and provide valuable feedback for schools.

The implementation of student chatbots is not without challenges. One significant concern is ensuring the privacy and security of student data. Schools must implement robust measures to protect sensitive information and comply with relevant regulations. Additionally, while chatbots can handle many routine inquiries, they may struggle with more complex or nuanced questions, necessitating a seamless handoff to human staff. There is also the challenge of ensuring that the chatbot's responses are accurate and up to date, requiring ongoing maintenance and updates. You may have read news articles about major school systems that adopted the chatbot process early on but ended up wasting valuable time and resources. Proceed with caution and care!

Both ChatGPT and Copilot Studio allow large systems to use institutional data to make publicly accessible chatbots. Anyone can create simulations and other interactive experiences with Claude or Canva AI, then publish them for wider use. This does require some technical expertise, and of course some testing. Individual schools or educators could use a tool like SchoolAI to create a chatbot for learners to access as well. A larger data set is most helpful because it will provide the most information. You may also wish to prompt the AI tool *not to* answer questions that are outside its data set. Remember, AI is programmed to make you happy. It will fabricate a solution if needed. Give it parameters to only answer within its data set and you'll have more success.

Learner-facing chatbots represent a significant augmentation to traditional support systems, offering immediate assistance while dramatically expanding the reach of educational resources beyond traditional time and staff constraints.

Personalized Learning Platforms

Personalized learning platforms are AI-driven systems that analyze individual learning styles, preferences, and performance data to create customized learning paths. Khanmigo is an example of this functionality. It's an AI-powered tutor and teaching assistant that uses advanced algorithms to provide customized support across a wide range of subjects, including math, science, humanities, and coding. Khanmigo analyzes each learner's interactions, performance, and progress to offer personalized recommendations and feedback. For instance, if a learner struggles with a particular math concept, Khanmigo can provide targeted practice problems and step-by-step explanations to help them improve. If a learner excels in a subject, Khanmigo can offer more challenging material to keep them engaged and motivated.

One of the key features of Khanmigo is its ability to provide real-time feedback and support. Learners can ask questions and receive immediate responses, which helps them understand concepts more deeply and correct mistakes on the spot. This instant feedback loop is so important for effective learning since it gives students a chance to address gaps in their understanding without waiting a week to get a quiz score back!

Khanmigo also gives educators insights into learner performance, which helps identify where students might need extra support (or enrichment, which has the added benefit of enhancing passion-based learning). However, despite these powerful functions, Khanmigo is still at the augmentation level of the SAMR model. It enhances traditional teaching methods with functional improvements. It adds to the learning experience by making it more interactive, responsive, and tailored to individual needs. But it is not redefining the tasks themselves. Personalized learning platforms upgrade traditional teaching methods with functional improvements: differentiated instruction that adapts in real time to each learner's progress.

It is important to remember that teachers play a significant role in guiding and supporting learners, and personalized learning platforms should be seen as a tool to enhance, rather than replace, the educator-learner relationship. After all, "a human touch in learning is incredibly powerful but horribly unscalable. An expert works individually with a learner to model, guide, provide feedback, challenge, and validate the learner's progress."[1] This creates profound impact that technology alone cannot replicate. AI-powered platforms help bridge this gap, extending the teacher's reach while preserving the essential human elements of education.

Personalized PD Plans and Virtual Coaching

School leaders and instructional coaches can leverage AI tools to create more effective, personalized professional development experiences for their teachers. Rather than replacing the human connection, AI enhances the coaching relationship by providing data-driven insights that inform more targeted conversations and support.

These AI-enhanced coaching relationships begin with tools that can analyze individual teachers' strengths, areas for improvement, and professional goals to help human mentors tailor development opportunities that are both relevant and impactful. Educators deserve to be able to plan their own professional growth in partnership with their leadership,

---

1   Micah Shippee, "AI in Education: A Focus on Pedagogy" (unpublished abstract, November 30, 2023), https://ssrn.com/abstract=4649752 or http://dx.doi.org/10.2139/ssrn.4649752.

and AI gives coaches the data they need to make those partnerships more meaningful.

When instructional coaches use AI-powered platforms, they can assess an educator's current skills and knowledge, then work together to identify specific training modules, resources, and workshops that align with professional development needs. If an educator excels in leading class discussions but needs improvement in integrating technology, the AI tool can provide the coach with targeted suggestions to discuss during their mentoring conversations.

AI also facilitates continuous feedback that enhances the human coaching relationship. By analyzing data from classroom observations, learner performance, and teacher self-assessments, AI tools can provide coaches with real-time insights and recommendations to discuss with teachers. This ongoing feedback loop helps human mentors guide educators to stay on track with their development goals and make adjustments as needed. These tools can also bridge some of the data gaps created by the misuse of generalized data. (Read the chapter on education in the amazing book *Weapons of Math Destruction* by Cathy O'Neil to learn more about this mess!)

AI also helps school leaders and coaches identify broader trends and needs within their teaching staff. By aggregating data from multiple educators, AI tools can highlight common areas where professional development is needed, allowing human leaders to plan and implement targeted training programs that benefit the entire staff. This data-driven approach ensures that professional development initiatives led by humans are aligned with the actual needs of the educators, making coaching conversations more effective and relevant.

It is essential for school leaders to ensure that the use of AI in human-led professional development is transparent and ethical. Educators should be informed about how their data is being used and be able to provide input on their development plans with their human coaches. Additionally, school leaders should ensure that AI recommendations are used as a supplement to, rather than a replacement for, human judgment and expertise in coaching relationships.

In terms of value, AI tools can offer human coaches real-time feedback and insights based on classroom interactions, helping mentors guide teachers to reflect on and improve their instructional strategies. For example, AI can analyze lesson recordings to provide detailed reports that coaches can discuss with teachers about learner engagement, the use of open-ended questions, the balance between teacher talk and student talk, and more. This immediate, data-driven feedback becomes incredibly valuable when filtered through the expertise and relationship-building skills of a human coach.

As a seasoned instructional coach, I am always wary of replacing the human connection in coaching relationships. However, I also understand that AI can make human coaches more effective by providing them with better data and insights to inform their mentoring conversations. Tools like TeachFX and AI Coach by Edthena can provide coaches with detailed analytics that enhance their face-to-face discussions with teachers. Remember that any school system can utilize AI data to inform human-led PD conversations through chatbots created in ChatGPT or Copilot Studio environments that coaches can reference during their mentoring sessions.

Before any of these AI-enhanced coaching tools are used in a school, the leadership team should ensure that they have created a supportive environment for vulnerability and growth. A culture of continuous improvement and openness to new technologies can encourage teachers to embrace AI-enhanced human coaching as a valuable resource rather than a daunting new approach.

Some educators may worry about data privacy or the accuracy of AI feedback shared with their human coaches. Administrators should ensure that robust data protection measures are in place and clearly communicate these safeguards to the staff. Additionally, emphasizing that AI enhances rather than replaces human judgment in coaching relationships can help alleviate fears about the technology.

While AI-enhanced coaching with human mentors provides valuable collaborative support, educators can also harness AI for completely independent professional growth through self-coaching approaches.

MODIFICATION

College/Career Guidance

Navigating college and career planning is often overwhelming for learners (and their home support people), as they must consider a wide range of factors, from college applications and scholarship opportunities to career pathways and skills development. Generative AI chatbots can play a role in supporting learners through this process by providing personalized, accessible guidance that complements the work of human counselors. While this might be helpful in lower schools (K–12), it will be super helpful at the higher education level, where there are more learners per counselor and a myriad of options to pursue.

Generative AI chatbots help students explore their college and career options based on their interests, academic performance, and long-term goals. By asking targeted questions, the chatbot can suggest potential colleges, majors, and career fields that align with the learner's strengths and goals. This personalized exploration helps learners identify opportunities they might not have considered otherwise. The chatbot can guide learners through the college application process by offering step-by-step instructions, reminders of important deadlines, and tips on how to strengthen their applications. It will provide tailored advice on writing personal statements, preparing for interviews, and selecting the right mix of extracurricular activities to enhance their applications. Additionally, the chatbot can help learners research financial aid options, scholarships, and grant opportunities that are relevant to their background and needs.

For learners who are more focused on entering the workforce directly after high school or pursuing vocational training, a chatbot can offer valuable insights into various career pathways. Chatbots provide information on job market trends, in-demand skills, and potential certifications or apprenticeships. By helping learners map out a clear plan, the chatbot can make the transition from school to career smoother and more informed. The AI chatbot is available anytime, allowing learners to explore their options and seek guidance when it's most convenient for them—and even in their preferred language and with audio and visual support. This accessibility is particularly valuable during critical periods such as application deadlines. The immediacy of the chatbot's responses will likely alleviate some of the stress and uncertainty associated with post-secondary decision-making.

Careerdekho is an AI-powered career guidance tool designed to help learners find the perfect career fit. It uses advanced algorithms to analyze a learner's skills, interests, and goals, providing personalized career recommendations. The tool considers various factors such as job market trends, salary potential, and job satisfaction to help learners make informed decisions about their career paths.

Coach is a platform that provides career coaching for university students and recent graduates. It offers structured, step-by-step guidance to help learners land their first internships and jobs. The platform focuses on clarity in career direction, networking skills, and creating action-oriented career plans.

ESAI.ai (Educational Support and AI) is a tool designed to enhance career readiness by focusing on the core competencies required for success in the workplace. It emphasizes skills such as communication, critical thinking, teamwork, and professionalism. ESAI provides detailed guidance on how to develop these competencies through various activities and real-world scenarios. By integrating these skills into the learning process, ESAI helps learners become well-rounded individuals who are prepared for the demands of the modern workforce.

Remember that generative AI models are trained on vast data sets that include content from various sources across the internet. These data sets can inadvertently reflect societal biases related to race, ethnicity, gender, and other identities. If not carefully monitored and managed, AI systems may perpetuate or even amplify these biases, leading to unfair or skewed outcomes in educational settings.

For example, a chatbot providing college and career advice might unintentionally favor certain careers or educational paths based on biased data. This could result in learners from underrepresented groups receiving less encouragement to pursue high-demand fields or prestigious colleges. Moreover, if the AI relies on data that predominantly reflects the experiences and values of certain groups, it may fail to provide relevant and accurate information for learners from diverse backgrounds.

Another concern is the potential for information bubbles. This is a phenomenon where hyper-personalization leads to learners receiving information from a narrow set of sources that align with their existing beliefs or preferences. This can prevent them from being exposed to divergent values, perspectives, and experiences that are fundamental for their intellectual and personal growth.

In an educational context, this could mean that a learner who has expressed an interest in a specific career path might only receive information that reinforces that choice, without being challenged to consider alternative options. Similarly, a learner might be directed toward reading materials or resources that align with their current worldview, missing out on the opportunity to engage with different or opposing viewpoints.

Instead of solely focusing on hyper-personalization, AI systems should be designed to encourage learners to explore a broader range of topics and perspectives. This could involve introducing learners to new ideas, challenging their assumptions, and prompting them to engage with content that offers alternative viewpoints. Of course, we can also provide some risk mitigation through human oversight. Educators and counselors can ensure learners receive well-rounded advice and that biases and information bubbles are identified and addressed.

> Behind every impactful educational technology tool are educators who saw its potential before others did. Your willingness to explore AI now puts you at the start of an educational movement that can benefit generations of learners.

Competency-Based Skill Building

Competency-based skill building is an approach focused on mastering specific skills or competencies at a learner's own pace before progressing. Unlike traditional models that emphasize time-based learning (one day, one week, one semester), competency-based education prioritizes proficiency in clear, measurable skills that students can apply in real-world contexts. This approach tailors learning to individual needs, ensuring that each learner acquires a skill before moving forward. By integrating AI, educators can further personalize this process, offering targeted resources and feedback that enhance learner outcomes and help prepare for future challenges.

NXTLVL is a powerful platform that supports students in developing competency-based skills through a variety of innovative and engaging methods. Central to its design are immersive missions led by an AI coach that help learners master skills like problem-solving, logical reasoning, decision-making, and leadership. These missions, structured as twenty-minute daily learning experiences, are both fun and effective. Personalized progression is integral to NXTLVL's approach. The platform provides weekly AI-generated highlights that offer learners specific analysis on their progress and guidance on their skills. AI coaches within NXTLVL act as intellectual sparring partners, offering advice in manageable chunks and prompting learners to reflect on their actions. This immersive approach enables learners to develop critical-thinking and problem-solving skills by addressing real-world challenges. NXTLVL incorporates a gamified element in the form of skill achievement badges.

A key focus is on the development of Power Skills, which include critical and creative thinking, effective communication, and collaboration. These skills are commonly accepted in the education community as essential for learners' future success.

Of course, learners can practice these types of skills outside of the NXTLVL app. Educators can set up simulations through any student-facing generative AI tool. Other systems won't have built-in analytics or interactivity on one platform, but they can provide one-time activities to work toward specific competencies.

We spend a lot of time in education talking about real-world skills and competencies. A platform like NXTLVL prepares learners for real-world scenarios without putting them in the situation quite yet. It reminds me of learning to drive a car in a simulator. Generative AI creates a responsive, interactive space in which learners can practice skills without real-world consequences.

Debate

Using AI to prepare for debates can spark deeper thinking through new tasks. In traditional debate prep, learners work in teams—partners or small groups—to practice communication skills, prepare for both sides, and imagine counterarguments and strategy. AI challenges learners' assumptions and presents diverse perspectives, encouraging critical thinking and the development of analytical skills. With a tool like DebateAI, learners must analyze AI-generated arguments, identify strengths and weaknesses, and develop well-reasoned responses. This process also improves their research skills, as they need to gather, evaluate, and synthesize information from various sources to support their arguments. AI provides instant feedback, helping learners refine their reasoning and communication skills in real time. It can also adjust the complexity of its responses based on the learner's level, ensuring that the debate remains challenging and educational.

Learners can also use any GPT to simulate a debate. While slightly complicated prompting is involved, a learner can ask a GPT to debate them on a topic, choose a side, wait for responses, and continue conversationally.

> **SAMPLE PROMPT**
>
> Create a debate simulation for a university-level political science course on the topic of "The impact of social media on democracy." You are debating against me, the student. First, assign me a role: either politician, journalist, or citizen. Provide me with background information for my role. Then assign me a side, pro or con. Next provide guidelines for conducting the debate with me. Begin by asking me for my opening statement. Wait for me to reply. Then respond with an opposing opening statement. Next, ask for one key argument. Wait for my reply, then respond with a rebuttal statement. Continue for three rounds. Then ask for a closing statement and respond with a closing statement. Score the debate and announce a winner. Provide me with feedback on how I can improve my arguments after the debate is complete.

Generative AI helps learners get exposure to a wide range of viewpoints, broadening their horizons and helping them develop empathy and a deeper understanding of complex issues. There might be points that did not appear in their research, that they did not practice with their teammates—and this better simulates what a true debate will be like. Debating with AI offers a safe and supportive environment for learners to practice their skills without fear of judgment, encouraging exploration and creativity. This practice enhances their ability to articulate thoughts clearly and persuasively and improves their listening and responding skills. Debates often require knowledge from multiple areas, promoting interdisciplinary learning and the integration of new tasks. Incorporating AI redefines debate preparation. Students are not just gathering information and writing arguments; they are actively engaging in a simulated debate environment that adapts to their responses, provides real-time feedback, and exposes them to a wide range of viewpoints. This renovation moves the activity beyond augmentation, making it an example of modification in the SAMR model.

Fluency Practice

Whether learners are exploring a new language, learning to read for the first time, or improving their read-aloud skills, AI has completely changed fluency practice. Many reading and speaking apps will listen to a speaker and give feedback on pronunciation, timing, and expression. These are excellent substitutes for practicing language or reading with a human, and they offer instant, anywhere feedback free from embarrassment.

Early readers require a huge amount of reading material for practice. However, assembling a collection that includes both narrative and nonfiction texts aligned with the learner's reading level and interests can be quite challenging.

AI tools like LitLab and Project Read can help by identifying appropriate texts within the classroom library or generating new ones that fit. These tools can focus on phonics skills and incorporate comprehension checks. They also ensure that instead of appearing only once, vocabulary words are reinforced across multiple texts.

With significant advancements in speech-to-text technology, tools such as Microsoft Reading Coach and Storywizard can listen to students read, provide real-time feedback, and create personalized learning paths based on the science of reading.

Taking things one step beyond traditional reading practice assignments, a read-aloud tool lets the learner generate the unique story they're going to practice and self-select their practice words. They can also earn badges, unlock new characters, personalize characters, insert themselves into the story (using platforms like Neon Wild), decide how the plot unfolds (which helps them learn about story structure), and even modify illustration styles.

Keep in mind that fluency tools like these are absolutely not just for children. They are for anyone who is learning to read in a language for the first time. In fact, my teenage daughter plans to use Reading Coach to practice her Spanish pronunciation at home.

AI-powered fluency practice tools modify the traditional read-aloud experience by providing immediate, judgment-free feedback and personalized guidance tailored to each student's specific needs. This technology creates a safe space for people of all ages to practice pronunciation and expression at their own pace, building confidence through private repetition before performing in front of peers or teachers—or a native speaker!

Identify Challenges

One especially interesting use of generative AI for educators is to help identify challenges in a lesson plan or unit. I see this as a modification, not a substitute for peer collaboration, because AI will have vastly more content in its data set than a person.

Educators can use generative AI to analyze a lesson plan and expose some common misconceptions learners may have about a lesson topic in advance. This allows educators to proactively address these issues, ensuring that learners have a clearer understanding from the outset.

> **SAMPLE PROMPT**
>
> As an educator preparing a lesson about space for third graders, I want to ensure that I address common misconceptions that learners might have about this topic. Please analyze the following lesson plan and identify potential misconceptions that third graders might hold. Consider misconceptions related to the sun, stars, planets, and the moon. Provide suggestions on how to address these misconceptions effectively within the lesson. Here is the lesson plan:
>
> Introduction to Space: Brief overview of the solar system, including the sun, planets, and the moon.
>
> The Sun and Stars: Explanation of what stars are, with a focus on the sun as a star.
>
> Planets: Description of the planets in our solar system, their characteristics, and their relative sizes and distances.
>
> The Moon: Discussion about the moon, its phases, and its relationship with Earth.

Sample response:

Potential Misconceptions to Address:

The sun is not a star because it looks different from other stars.

Stars are only visible at night.

Earth is flat or shaped like a plate.

The moon produces its own light.

Mars is hot because it is red.

Planets cannot be seen without a telescope.

Suggestions for Addressing Misconceptions:

Use visual aids and comparisons to explain that the sun is a star and why it appears different from other stars.

> Explain that stars are always present in the sky, but the sun's brightness during the day makes them invisible.
>
> Use globes and models to demonstrate Earth's round shape.
>
> Clarify that the moon reflects the sun's light and does not produce its own light.
>
> Discuss the actual temperatures of planets and why Mars appears red.
>
> Show images and videos of planets visible to the naked eye and explain how they can be seen without a telescope.
>
> By addressing these misconceptions, the lesson will provide a clearer and more accurate understanding of space for third graders.

A GPT can also help identify some obstacles in the lesson plans that educators may not consider independently. Educators can then adjust the lesson plan based on these obstacles, transforming the traditional approach to lesson planning into a more dynamic and responsive process.

SAMPLE PROMPT

> I'd like to have my third graders create a model of the solar system. What are some challenges my students may have with this activity?

Sample response:

> Creating a model of the solar system can be an exciting and educational activity for third graders, but it does come with several challenges that educators should be prepared to address:
>
> Understanding scale and proportion: One of the biggest challenges is helping learners grasp the vast differences in size and distance between the planets. For example, the distance

from the sun to Neptune is nearly three billion miles, which is difficult to represent accurately in a classroom setting. Simplifying these concepts without losing accuracy can be tricky.

Material selection and availability: Choosing the right materials to represent the planets and their relative sizes can be challenging. Learners might struggle with finding or creating materials that accurately depict the planets' sizes and distances. Using beads, string, or even sidewalk chalk can help, but ensuring these materials are available and suitable for the project is essential.

Spatial awareness: Learners may find it difficult to visualize and arrange the planets in a way that accurately represents their positions in the solar system. This can be particularly challenging in a confined space like a classroom. Deciding whether to focus on the scale of planet sizes or distances can help manage this challenge.

Accuracy and detail: Ensuring that the model is scientifically accurate while still being understandable for third graders can be a delicate balance. Learners might oversimplify or misunderstand certain aspects, such as the fact that the moon reflects the sun's light instead of producing its own.

Engagement and motivation: Keeping all learners engaged throughout the project can be challenging, especially if some find the task too difficult or not challenging enough. Providing clear instructions, breaking the project into manageable steps, and incorporating interactive elements can help maintain interest.

Collaboration and teamwork: If the project is done in groups, managing collaboration can be a challenge. Ensuring that all learners participate equally and that group dynamics are positive is key for the success of the project.

By anticipating these challenges and planning accordingly, educators can help learners create a successful and educational model of the solar system. Using AI tools to provide additional support and resources can also enhance the learning experience and address some of these challenges effectively.

This type of feedback can be incredibly useful. Some educators may not work in environments where they can ask a veteran educator for support, or they might not have a colleague with a similar teaching assignment. Seeing obstacles to lessons in advance gives the educator a chance to adjust the lesson, requirements, or approach ahead of time, which ensures a more successful experience for the learners.

An educator might follow this type of conversation with a GPT by asking for specific feedback on ideas they've had.

> **SAMPLE PROMPT**
>
> I was thinking of having each student share their model with the class through a short presentation. I'm worried it will get boring, but I want my students to practice their presentation skills. What could I do differently?

Sample response:

To keep the presentations engaging while allowing learners to practice their presentation skills, you can incorporate a few creative strategies:

Interactive elements: Encourage learners to include interactive elements in their presentations. For example, they could ask the class questions, conduct a quick quiz, or involve their peers in a small activity related to their model. This keeps the audience engaged and makes the presentation more dynamic.

Use of technology: Allow learners to use technology to enhance their presentations. They could create a short video or animation to accompany their model, use a digital slideshow with interesting facts and images, or even incorporate augmented reality (AR) to bring their models to life. Tools like Google Slides, Prezi, or AR apps can make their presentations more visually appealing and interactive.

Role-playing: Have learners present their models as if they are space explorers, scientists, or news reporters. This role-playing aspect can make the presentations more fun and engaging as learners adopt different personas and storytelling techniques.

Peer feedback: Incorporate a peer feedback session where learners can give and receive constructive feedback on their presentations. This not only helps improve their presentation skills but also keeps the audience actively involved.

Group presentations: Instead of individual presentations, consider having learners work in small groups to present their models. This can reduce the number of presentations and allow for more in-depth exploration of each model. Group work also supports collaboration and communication skills.

Themed presentations: Assign different themes or aspects of the solar system to each learner or group. For example, one group could focus on the inner planets, another on the outer planets, and another on the sun and its role in the solar system. This variety keeps the content fresh and interesting for the audience.

Creative formats: Encourage learners to present their models in creative formats such as a news broadcast, a talk show, or a documentary. This can make the presentations more entertaining and memorable.

By incorporating these strategies, you can ensure that the presentations remain engaging and educational while also providing learners with valuable opportunities to practice and improve their presentation skills.

This type of lesson plan support can completely change the task of teacher preparation from just churning out new lesson ideas to critically evaluating them. The time is spent differently—instead of coming up with ideas, educators are thinking through the impact of those ideas and asking AI to assist, with its vast knowledge set, by providing information on potential problems and solutions. Ultimately this type of lesson preparation is creating better learning environments!

Mental Health Support

This is another hot topic! Metacognitive skills play an important role in guiding learners to become functional members of society, yet they are often overlooked in traditional education settings. Metacognitive skills include self-awareness, cultivating a growth mindset, seeking and integrating feedback, setting and pursuing goals, and monitoring progress. These are essential for people to thrive both academically and personally. However, many learners struggle to develop these competencies on their own. It can be difficult to target them in a classroom setting given competing initiatives like core curriculum and behavior.

Generative AI is one step toward a solution to this gap. It provides personalized, context-aware support that acts like an empathetic mentor. Learners can use chatbots to receive real-time guidance and encouragement in things like self-efficacy and resilience. SchoolAI's Spaces offering is one example of how AI can assist learners in creating study plans, adopting effective exam-taking strategies, and making informed decisions about their learning. This and similar AI-supported systems go beyond traditional to-do lists and study aids by understanding each learner's unique context, learning preferences, and challenges.

Robin Lowell, an amazing educator and expert in executive function, is often quoted as saying, "Kids would rather go without than stand out." Learners who are struggling with mental health and executive function issues are the least likely to shout for support. These learners can be well served by taking the first step toward the support they need through an empathetic, nonjudgmental, always-available tool that feels somewhat like a friend.

AI tools like Woebot Health and Koko offer learners 24/7 anonymous mental health support, which can be especially valuable for those who may feel uncomfortable reaching out to a human counselor. AI-powered chatbots like EdSights and Mainstay provide a safe, nonjudgmental environment where learners can talk about their feelings, practice social skills, and receive advice and encouragement. These tools can also help connect learners who are experiencing similar challenges, which can cultivate a sense of community and mutual support desperately missing from these learners' lives. Additionally, these tools track patterns that may signal a decline in mental health. The human intervention here is key. We must enable school staff to recommend professional help or notify a designated support person when needed.

I truly hope generative AI doesn't take away from the human element in education. Schools using AI tutors might miss out on the importance of educators who truly care for their learners, inspire them, and demonstrate what it means to be a well-rounded adult. Ideally, AI should help free up more time for educators to focus on building genuine human connections. To strengthen the community at the core of our schools, we need to prioritize learning that supports not just academic growth but also the mental health and well-being of our students.

See a TikTalkWalk about this here!

Self-Coaching

AI offers educators the opportunity to engage in completely independent professional development through self-coaching. In this approach, teachers take full ownership of their reflection process, using AI tools to analyze their own practice without the need for a human mentor or coach to be present.

In self-coaching, a teacher records the audio of a lesson and uses AI tools to get feedback on skills. This is not a substitution for a supervisor's observation or a human coaching relationship. Much like learner use of chatbots helps them feel safer revealing personal information, AI-powered self-observation changes the self-reflection task entirely. Educators using AI-powered observation tools for self-coaching are not subject to human judgment. They likely feel more freedom to teach naturally without the pressure of an evaluation or the presence of another adult. Even their learners are likely more relaxed without an additional person in the class environment hovering and taking notes.

AI tools like TeachFX and Edthena can analyze recorded lessons to provide insights on various teaching skills. For example, an AI tool might highlight instances where a teacher could have allowed more time for students to think before answering, or it could suggest alternative strategies for managing classroom disruptions. This immediate, data-driven feedback helps educators reflect on their practices and make informed adjustments to improve their effectiveness.

AI-powered self-coaching promotes continuous professional development. Unlike traditional coaching, which may be limited by time and availability of mentors, AI tools are accessible anytime and can provide ongoing support. This allows educators to engage in self-reflection and professional growth at their own pace, building a culture of lifelong learning. These tools can focus on self-selected frameworks to support school-wide implementations.

AI tools can identify patterns and trends in teaching practices that might not be evident through self-observation alone. For instance, an AI system could analyze multiple recordings to detect consistent strengths and areas for improvement, offering a comprehensive view of an educator's performance over time. This holistic perspective enables teachers to set targeted goals and track their progress more effectively.

Self-coaching does not have to only exist in audio and video recordings. Many educators may not have access to the devices necessary to use these platforms. Instead, an educator might engage in AI-powered coaching by engaging with a generative AI teaching adviser. This reduces the need for in-person coaching (and even technical support) and lets the educator receive instant support. Check out a platform like EduGPT for a great example of chatbots designed to help any educator in any situation. The app's AI Faculty list includes different grade levels, platform experts, topic bots, and more. These bots are designed to give tailored recommendations based on a specific data set for that topic. While far from perfect, this is a step toward equitable support for all educators regardless of their school funding and staffing model. Tools like Teaching Lab and CoTeach will take existing lessons and give the educator improvement suggestions. This might include pacing, format, activities, or even foundational skills that might have been missed. By engaging with an AI adviser, educators might become more comfortable with a reflective and proactive teaching culture. This collaboration can enhance individual growth and contribute to a more innovative teaching community.

No, this absolutely does not replace human instructional coaches. While AI advisers offer valuable data-driven insights and can significantly enhance the self-coaching process for educators, the role of human instructional coaches remains indispensable. Human coaches bring a depth of understanding, empathy, and contextual awareness that AI cannot replicate. They can interpret nuanced classroom dynamics, provide emotional support, and build trusting relationships that nurture professional growth. Human coaches can tailor their feedback and strategies to the unique needs and personalities of individual teachers, something AI, with its reliance on data patterns, may struggle to achieve. AI should be seen as a powerful supplement to, rather than a replacement for, the human touch in instructional coaching.

Talk to a Character

This has been one of my favorite activities since I first learned about SchoolAI. There are premade spaces for this purpose, or you can create your own. But the impact of having a "conversation" with a historical character, book character, or even a person in the world today is real. (Do I have reservations about this? Yes. More soon. Let's focus on the possibilities first.)

There are many benefits to this activity. First, AI-driven interactions can make learning about a topic or person more engaging and enjoyable. Learners will be more interested in the content because it feels realistic, and the conversation is responsive and personal. Characters "come to life" through the power of generative AI. Learners are also likely to have a deeper understanding of historical events, scientific topics, or literary themes. They can ask questions and receive detailed responses, which helps build a more nuanced understanding. Because AI can adapt the interactions based on the learner's comprehension level and interest, students are less likely to lose interest, feel overwhelmed, or get stuck in difficult text. With educator support, learners are encouraged to think more critically and ask probing questions. There is no embarrassment here for asking the "wrong" question! Learners become active participants instead of passive recipients. This approach might also help them better visualize big concepts, settings, or environments. They will get descriptions to support their learning at their own pace and level. AI-generated conversations can be more accessible too. Learners who struggle with traditional reading assignments may be more likely to finish an interactive conversation.

This is a huge shift from reading a paragraph or watching a video about a topic, person, or theme. The task is redefined. Educators can still pose guiding questions, but the learners have more control over how they approach finding the answers. In SchoolAI, for example, educators set the boundaries on these conversations and guide the bots through the settings to respond to certain questions or even avoid certain topics. AI will gently guide the learners back to the point of the conversation while acknowledging their personal approach.

I used SchoolAI to allow middle school students (ages eleven to thirteen) to learn more about different women in history during

Women's History Month. I set up four different spaces with women to interview. In a class of thirty students, it was a surprisingly even split between the four women. I was really interested to see who the students chose and why. I loved being able to see their conversations with my educator insights and talk to students individually to follow up on any off-task behavior or extra thoughtful questions. While I'm writing this, SchoolAI has about thirty prebuilt historical characters for learners to interact with. Of course, you can always make your own—and you should!

EduGPT's AI Faculty section includes tons of different characters. Many of these are meant to help learners with assignments, but there are a few historical characters as well.

OK, I promised to get back to my concerns. Let's begin with algorithmic bias. AI systems can inadvertently perpetuate biases present in their training data. This can lead to biased responses that reflect stereotypes or unfair assumptions about certain groups. I also have concerns about representation. Ensure that the AI includes diverse perspectives and accurately represents different cultures and histories. This is crucial in a diverse classroom setting to avoid reinforcing existing biases. Educators should be aware of biases and actively work to moderate them by providing diverse and balanced prompts as they create the bots and regularly reviewing AI outputs for fairness. Hallucinations can confuse students and undermine the credibility of the educational content. It's essential to cross-check AI-generated information with reliable sources. Review the responses learners are receiving and spot-check for factual information so you can correct any errors.

Finally, anytime coders program an algorithm to represent a human, I have concerns. In 2022, an AI company was pleased to share that they used some vodcast footage of me being interviewed and changed my voice to speak different languages. I was not happy. In my opinion, the company misrepresented my voice without my permission, and I believe my voice is my property. While the technology is amazing, and I would have been excited if they had asked me first, I was unimpressed with the way their marketing pitch was handled. I feel somewhat the same about bringing a character to life, especially a real person from history. We don't know how that person would actually respond, and we must be extra careful that AI doesn't misrepresent their voice. Responsible AI is important here, and helping learners see the purpose behind the activity while understanding its pitfalls is paramount.

Thought Partner

Speaking of getting help, giving educators access to an AI-powered colleague (a.k.a. chatbot) can be useful. I love that EduGPT has created personas for different age levels, classes, and topics. Learners can select a chatbot that is designed to help educators with teaching seventh-grade English, eighth-grade science, or even a language. What's cool about EduGPT is that schools can configure their own AI portals, ensuring that the tools align with their specific educational goals, standards, and policies. Wouldn't it be great if your school system had a prebuilt chatbot just for your content area and learners that localized the content and worked off existing standards? Educators could ask for help with the lesson, how to teach a certain topic, or anything. This is next-level support compared to simply asking a GPT for help with an assignment. These tools have been specifically coded with a data set for that purpose, and they often have preset parameters in the background.

EduGPT provides sample prompts to help educators get started, and it includes technical support as well. I love the idea of getting instant help with edtech tools educators are using in schools: Canva, Canvas, Teams, Google Classroom, Zoom, Schoology, Pear Deck, and more all have their own chatbot assistant to give educators a boost on technical support.

The English teacher assistants in EduGPT have a variety of writing styles to use: comedic, satirical, biographical, narrative, poetic, and about twenty more. This enhances the outputs to match a particular mode, which can be even more interesting to read. I asked an assistant for help understanding satire and to suggest examples I could use with my class.

The most common time in the entire world for educators to be lesson planning is . . . you guessed it, Sunday evenings. Your fellow educators are not going to be around and available then. They're surfing Pinterest boards and searching for their own ideas. AI has completely changed the way educators can get support, and I'm here for it.

AI-powered thought partners modify the traditional planning process by providing educators with immediate, expertise-informed feedback that would typically require scheduling time with a colleague or instructional coach. It's a free, on-demand, collaborative thinking space allowing teachers to refine their ideas at their own convenience, creating a bridge between independent planning and human collaboration.

CONCLUSION

Artificial intelligence offers amazing opportunities to provide the personalized support that educators have long known students need but have struggled to deliver despite their best efforts. By implementing AI tools across the SAMR framework, we can move from basic support enhancements to fundamentally transformed learning experiences that adapt to each student's unique needs.

Return for a moment to my seventh-grade classroom, where Students 1, 2, 3, and 4 represent just a small sample of the varied learning needs present in any educational setting. With AI-powered support systems in place, Student 1 can access real-time translation and language scaffolding, Student 2 can pursue enrichment pathways that keep her engaged (and maybe even let her prep for volleyball tryouts), Student 3 can receive content through audio and visual formats that accommodate his dyslexia, and Student 4 can demonstrate her understanding through alternative assessment approaches that bypass her writing anxiety—and I'd definitely sneak her some snacks until lunchtime.

This level of personalization isn't just about academic outcomes, although those certainly improve when instruction matches student needs. It's also about dignity, engagement, and equity. When students receive appropriate support, they experience education as a system designed with them in mind, rather than one they must struggle to fit into. This shift in experience can alter and improve attitudes toward learning, build confidence, and even encourage the sense of belonging that research consistently identifies as critical for educational success.

For teachers, AI support tools don't diminish their role. They simply expand their impact. By handling routine support functions and providing initial personalization layers, AI frees educators to focus on the aspects of teaching that most require human insight. It gives time back for building relationships, facilitating meaningful discussions, providing emotional support, and helping students make connections between concepts. Technology becomes an amplifier of teacher capacity rather than a replacement for teacher expertise.

For students, AI support creates a safety net that catches them before they fall too far behind while simultaneously offering pathways to push beyond grade-level expectations when they're ready. This combination of remediation and enrichment, provided as needed, helps every learner progress steadily rather than get frustrated by material that's either too challenging or not challenging enough.

For administrators and school leaders, AI support systems offer ways to address persistent equity gaps, provide specialized services at scale, and collect actionable data about where additional human resources might be most effectively deployed.

As you implement these support approaches in your own context, remember that the goal isn't to automate support but to humanize it. Our goal when using AI supports is to make learning more responsive, more accessible, and more effective for each unique person. The most powerful AI support systems don't stand alone but integrate seamlessly with human relationships and expertise, creating an educational environment where technology and humanity enhance each other.

In the next chapter, we'll move from supporting learning to analyzing it, exploring how AI can help gather and interpret data during implementation. While support ensures students have what they need to succeed, analysis helps us understand if that success is being achieved and how we might adjust our approach.

8

ANALYZE

IMAGINE A CLASSROOM WHERE EVERY student knows exactly which skills they've mastered and which areas need more attention. Picture a teacher who can instantly identify not just who's struggling but precisely where and why, seeing patterns across assignments that would otherwise remain hidden. Envision a school leader who can spot emerging trends across hundreds of data points, making proactive decisions rather than reactive ones.

Data has always been important in education. Schools are filled with data from test scores, attendance records, behavioral patterns, and engagement metrics. But the sheer volume of information and the complexity of analysis means that most educational data is underutilized. I remember digging through an overwhelming amount of data when I was teaching fourth grade. I really wanted to know which reading skills my students needed help in, and I was prepared to categorize every assessment question and provide individualized reteaching and practice based on each child's needs. (I was young, energetic, and had twenty-four students. Even then, it wasn't a sustainable practice.) Students sometimes receive grades but are uncertain about their exact strengths and growth areas. Administrators compile mandatory reports but rarely have opportunities to extract meaningful insights from the numbers.

The result? Many students, teachers, and schools operate in what might be called survival mode. This is functional but far below our true potential. A well-managed school might never recognize the systemic opportunity that could upgrade it into an exceptional one.

This is where artificial intelligence can really make an impact. AI doesn't just process data faster. It also discovers connections, identifies patterns, and generates insights that would remain invisible to even the most diligent human analyst constrained by time and cognitive limitations. Through AI-powered analysis, we can move beyond "good enough" to discover what students, educators, and schools are truly capable of achieving.

The SAMR framework provides a road map for this:

At the *substitution* level, AI can analyze data and summarize content more efficiently than traditional methods, saving valuable time while maintaining the basic analytical process.

At the *augmentation* level, AI enhances analysis through attendance pattern recognition, meeting summaries that capture nuances a human might miss, predictive analytics that forecast future trends, and research assistance that draws connections across diverse sources.

At the *modification* level, AI enhances the analytical process itself, enabling forms of pattern recognition, correlation discovery, and data visualization that fundamentally change how we understand educational processes and outcomes.

This chapter explores practical applications of AI-powered analysis for teachers, students, and administrators. Instead of drowning in data or making decisions based on limited information, everyone in the educational ecosystem can use these tools to gain deeper insights, identify opportunities for growth, and push beyond perceived limitations.

By uncovering the specific areas where individuals and institutions can improve, AI analysis creates a pathway to personalized rigor. This pathway can challenge each student, educator, and school to reach their unique potential rather than settle for standardized expectations. The question shifts from "Are we doing well enough?" to "What are we truly capable of achieving?"

> The AI optimist recognizes that data analysis in education isn't about reducing students to numbers but about seeing each learner more fully. With AI handling complex pattern recognition through massive data sets, educators can discover more about their students and how to support them.

SUBSTITUTION

Data Analysis

Generative AI can significantly enhance the capabilities of school administrators and principals in data analysis. Using AI algorithms, they can sift through huge amounts of data to identify trends, patterns, and insights that would be time-consuming to uncover on their own. For instance, AI can analyze student performance metrics to pinpoint areas where interventions are needed or evaluate the effectiveness of a new curriculum. Generative AI can also quickly generate reports and visualizations to communicate a story. Conditional formatting has been in Microsoft Excel for a long time, and it's also in Google Sheets. Use conditional formatting to quickly surface data trends through color. It's easy and beautiful!

Learners can also benefit from these data analysis capabilities to take ownership of their learning journey. Students can upload their own assessment results to a spreadsheet and use AI to help identify patterns in their performance across different subjects or skill areas. For example, a high school student might use AI to analyze their quiz scores over a semester, revealing that they consistently score lower on questions requiring specific types of mathematical reasoning. The AI could generate personalized visualizations showing their strengths and growth areas, helping them target their study efforts more effectively. I did something like this teaching middle school writing skills; students individually tracked their scores in each of the six traits of writing and set weekly focus goals that they were then evaluated against the following week. AI would have made this task so much simpler!

AI can also help students develop critical data literacy skills by explaining the patterns it identifies in approachable language. When a student asks, "Why did this pattern appear in our data?" or "What might explain this outlier?" the AI can suggest possible interpretations while encouraging the student to consider alternative explanations. This support-based approach to data analysis builds students' confidence with reasoning skills and may even allow them to be more capable of recognizing data-driven claims in their daily lives.

AI analysis tools can reveal hidden patterns of inequity in educational outcomes that might otherwise remain invisible. For instance, AI might identify that certain assessment methods systematically disadvantage specific student groups or that resource allocation unintentionally favors some programs over others. However, we must also ensure that the metrics and benchmarks built into these systems don't encode existing biases or deficit perspectives about certain student populations.

AI-powered data analysis tools substitute for traditional manual methods by quickly identifying patterns and generating visualizations that would otherwise require significant time and expertise. This efficiency allows educators and students to focus on interpreting insights rather than managing spreadsheets, making data-informed decisions more accessible to everyone in the educational community.

Summaries of Presentations or Spreadsheets

Any text-based generative AI tool does a great job at summarizing text. But to get help with your presentations or spreadsheets, you'll need to use generative AI that's connected to your files. That's where the enterprise tools come in handy. Ask ChatGPT, Gemini, or Copilot to summarize content of a document or PDF so you can quickly review a resource to prepare for a meeting. The tool should also give footnotes or link to portions of the file so you can dig deeper into slides or cells that need some human review.

In PowerPoint, you can add an extension for ChatGPT or use built-in Copilot to summarize the file without leaving PowerPoint. Recently when I needed to prepare for a presentation at short notice, I used AI to summarize forty slides that someone else had created. The summary identified key points and flagged several slides that I needed to pay attention to, allowing me to focus my limited preparation time where it mattered most. This approach helped me engage in the discussion despite the time constraints.

You can also use the AI-generated summary feature to gain a general understanding of a whole document. It's a little like reading the back cover of a book before you purchase it! Having an upfront idea of what to expect in a document can make it easier to read and digest.

AI-powered summary functions substitute for time-consuming manual review processes, condensing extensive information while preserving links to source material for deeper investigation. This allows educators and leaders to quickly review the content without sacrificing the ability to examine specific details when necessary.

AUGMENTATION

Attendance Reporting

Tracking attendance in a school system ensures that learners are accounted for and safe. And regular attendance is a strong predictor of academic success. Learners who attend school consistently are more likely to perform well academically and graduate on time. Monitoring attendance helps identify patterns of absenteeism, which can signal underlying issues such as health problems, family difficulties, or disengagement from school. Early identification allows for timely interventions to support the student.

While I am not a fan of perfect attendance awards, attendance data helps schools allocate resources effectively. For example, if a particular grade or subgroup shows high absenteeism rates, schools can target support and resources to those areas. This is where artificial intelligence can really shine!

AI tools significantly enhance attendance tracking by automating the process and providing real-time data analysis. For instance, AI-powered facial recognition systems can quickly and accurately record student attendance as learners enter the classroom, eliminating the need for manual roll calls and reducing errors. AI algorithms can also analyze attendance data to identify patterns and trends such as frequent absences or tardiness, alerting administrators to potential issues. This allows for timely interventions and support for learners who may be struggling. AI can even integrate attendance data with other student information systems, providing a comprehensive view of student engagement and performance. This empowers schools to allocate resources more effectively and possibly address the root causes of absenteeism.

Your student information system may already have AI-powered attendance tracking. If not, look for a secure, data-protected attendance tool. Taskade has a list of AI generators that are worth checking out, including ones for attendance.

Alternatively, upload a spreadsheet of attendance data to a GPT and ask it to analyze the data and look for trends. You can also use conditional formatting in Microsoft Excel or Google Sheets. Conditional formatting uses AI-powered data analysis to provide a visual representation of the data in the worksheet. It just takes a few steps and can highlight information otherwise missed by a human staring at rows of numbers.

AI-powered attendance tracking augments traditional monitoring systems by automatically identifying patterns and trends that might otherwise go unnoticed amid rows of data. These tools allow administrators and teachers to intervene earlier and more effectively, potentially changing routine recordkeeping into a proactive support system for student success.

Meeting Summaries

School administrators, leaders, heads, coordinators, and specialists attend a lot of meetings—meetings where not everyone's input is required. Some attendees are there just to ask questions or get information they can take it back to their own teams. Attending live may not always be necessary. Traditionally, someone missing an in-person meeting might get notes from a colleague who did attend. In a substitution model, people use recording and transcription tools, then read the transcription. At the augmentation level, we want artificial intelligence to provide functional improvement. Meeting recap AI tools do just that.

These tools do more than keep track of the notes—they can provide insights, action items, follow-up notes, speaker analytics, searchable content, suggested resources, and more. They can perform a variety of tasks during and after the meeting and integrate with your meeting tool to record and save, transcribe, take notes, summarize key points, generate meeting minutes, identify action items, and ensure data security. I use Microsoft Teams for virtual meetings, and I've used it to join in-person meetings as well (physical Teams meeting rooms are designed for just this). Copilot within Teams provides me with a ton of in- and post-meeting features. If a participant joins a meeting more than five minutes late, they'll receive a notification to get a meeting summary automatically inside Copilot. AI-powered features in virtual meetings enhance productivity by providing tools like real-time transcription, intelligent meeting summaries, action item tracking, and agenda creation. These systems automate repetitive tasks, facilitate clearer follow-up communication, and improve collaboration with tools for accurate note-taking, task management, and follow-up reminders.

Otter and Fireflies.ai are just two popular tools that I often see used on Zoom calls. You might also check out Fathom, ClickUp, and any AI supplement that's built into your virtual meeting platform. As always, make sure you're using a data-protected tool with school meetings!

If you don't have access to AI-powered meeting notes but do have access to transcription, try copying and pasting the transcript into a GPT and asking for the information you need.

Predictive Analytics

Analyzing learner data to predict who might need extra help is incredibly powerful. Predictive analytics tools examine patterns in learners' work, attendance, and engagement, providing an opportunity for educators and school leaders to use early intervention strategies. AI-powered predictive analytics enhance the traditional approach to monitoring and supporting learner progress. Instead of relying solely on assessment data or anecdotal evidence like educator observations, AI tools offer continuous, real-time insight into each learner's performance that combines multiple data sets across classes, platforms, and systems.

For educators, this means having a clearer picture of their learners' needs without the extensive manual analysis of data. The AI system can highlight learners who might benefit from additional tutoring, differentiated instruction, or enrichment activities. This enables educators to focus their efforts where they are most needed, making their instruction more effective and personalized.

Learners benefit too. Those who need extra help can receive targeted support before they fall too far behind, and learners who would thrive with additional challenges can be given opportunities to go beyond the class norms.

There is an argument that predictive analytics can help reduce educational inequalities by identifying and addressing learning gaps early. However, it is important to be mindful of the potential biases in AI algorithms. Teachers should use predictive analytics as a tool to complement their professional judgment, ensuring that decisions are made with a holistic understanding of each learner's context and working together with school counselors and other specialists.

Microsoft Teams for Education offers a built-in analytics tool called Insights. It gives all sorts of data to the educator and provides real-time information on anything happening inside the team space. Many school systems use Power BI to visualize large amounts of data. Educators with access to Microsoft 365 Education can also create Power BI dashboards to do this. It's simple to get started—just upload a spreadsheet and ask Power BI to visualize it for you! Many of the major LMS platforms offer combined analytics as well, and third-party apps like Edmentum can be helpful for collating data from multiple locations into one space.

AI-powered predictive analytics augment monitoring systems by identifying subtle patterns across multiple data sources that human analysis might miss, enabling more personalized and timely interventions. This enhancement adds capacity to anticipate student needs and transforms reactive support systems into proactive ones, potentially catching struggling students before they fall behind and identifying those ready for additional challenges.

Research Assistance

AI tools are changing the research process by providing learners with powerful capabilities to gather, analyze, and synthesize information. These tools significantly enhance traditional research tasks, making the process more efficient and thorough for the learner. Gone are the days of card catalogs—but also gone are the days of choosing the first hit in a list of web search results.

Learners need to understand how to search and what their search results might mean in relation to their search terms. Microsoft's Search Coach helps with this. It's designed to encourage learners to develop effective search strategies and critically evaluate their search results. Search Coach provides a guided, supportive environment to practice and refine their digital literacy skills. One of its key features is advice on how to compose efficient search queries—a task that many struggle with. Search Coach provides tips on how to structure queries to yield the best results. For example, it suggests using specific keywords, Boolean operators, and filters to narrow down search results. Search Coach also helps learners evaluate the reliability and relevance of their search results. It explains the significance of different domain types (.edu, .org, .gov, etc.) and how they can impact the trustworthiness of a source. As learners use Search Coach, they receive real-time feedback and tips. For example, if I search "Are cats better than dogs?" Search Coach will alert me that my question is biased, explain that it will present biased search results, and give a suggestion for a more neutral search, like "Compare the ownership commitment for cats and dogs." By understanding these distinctions, learners can make more informed decisions about which sources to use in their research. If a search query is too broad or too narrow, the tool will provide suggestions on how to refine it. This immediate feedback helps learners adjust their strategies on the fly, leading to more effective and efficient searches. While Search Coach isn't generative AI, it is powered by AI, and it's a solid step toward AI literacy for younger learners.

AI-powered search engines, such as Bing and Google Scholar, can help learners quickly find relevant academic articles, papers, and resources. These tools use advanced algorithms to filter and rank search results, ensuring that learners access high-quality and pertinent information. AI tools like ResearchRabbit can suggest related articles and papers based on the initial search, helping learners discover new sources they might have missed.

Learners can use a GPT (or a browser extension like Brisk or Copilot) as a summarization tool to condense long articles and papers into concise summaries. Many AI tools for education offer text summarization as well and will even give teachers an option to select the reading level. Diffit does a great job of this. Providing summaries allows learners to grasp the key points and arguments quickly, saving time and making it easier to manage large volumes of information. These tools can also highlight important sections and provide an overview of the main findings, helping learners synthesize information from multiple sources more effectively. I'm not recommending that learners skip reading research papers. I am recommending, however, that we give learners the opportunity to reduce their cognitive load and support executive function by guiding them to use tools that allow them to choose which resources demand their full attention, which can be skimmed, and which should be skipped entirely. That's a skill we all need!

Learners need help organizing their research results too. AI tools can assist them in organizing and managing their references. Citation tools can automatically generate citations in various formats, create bibliographies, and store research materials in an organized manner. This not only saves time but also ensures that learners maintain accurate and consistent references throughout their work. Many citation tools have a cost associated with them, but learners in higher education may find value in buying a personal license to help them stay organized.

For learners involved in data-driven research, AI tools like IBM Watson and Google Cloud offer advanced data analysis capabilities. These tools can process large data sets, identify patterns, and generate insights that would be difficult to uncover manually. By using AI for data analysis, learners can enhance the depth and rigor of their research, leading to more robust and reliable findings. By integrating AI tools into their research process, students can enhance their efficiency and the quality of their work. These tools provide valuable support in gathering, analyzing, and synthesizing information, helping learners to conduct more thorough and effective research.

CONCLUSION

Artificial intelligence can change educational analysis from a limited and retrospective process into a powerful tool for growth and improvement. By implementing AI analytical tools across the SAMR framework, we move from basic data processing to deep insight generation that pushes students, educators, and schools beyond what was previously possible.

The power of AI analysis lies in its ability to personalize rigor. AI can identify the precise areas where each student can stretch, where each teacher can refine their practice, and where each school can optimize its systems. A targeted approach replaces generic expectations with specific, actionable paths toward excellence tailored to individual strengths, challenges, and circumstances.

For students, AI analysis reveals not just what they've learned but how they learn best. It identifies patterns in their work that might indicate untapped potential in specific areas or approaches that could overcome persistent challenges. Rather than settle for "good enough" grades, students can understand exactly what adjustments would help them achieve at higher levels. Remember the old "Needs improvement" rating on report cards? Let's turn that into specific guidance like "Incorporating more counterarguments would strengthen your position papers."

For teachers, AI analysis changes assessment from a time-consuming obligation into a rich source of instructional insight. By quickly identifying patterns across student work, highlighting unexpected connections between concepts, and generating visualizations that make complex data interpretable, these tools enable educators to refine their teaching with unprecedented precision. A teacher might discover that while most students grasp a concept when it's presented visually, a significant subset of the class learns better through narratives. This insight leads to more targeted instructional approaches that serve all learners.

For administrators and school leaders, AI analysis provides a comprehensive view of school operations that can reveal both systemic challenges and hidden opportunities. Pattern recognition across attendance, achievement, engagement, and other metrics might highlight previously unnoticed factors affecting student success, allowing for proactive intervention rather than reactive response. This level of insight enables more efficient resource allocation, more effective professional development, and more impactful school improvement initiatives.

Maybe most importantly, AI analysis creates a common language of growth that connects all members of the educational community. When students, teachers, and administrators all have access to meaningful, actionable data about their performance, communication becomes more productive and focused on specific improvements rather than generic goals.

As you implement these analytical approaches in your own context, remember that the goal isn't simply to collect more data or generate more reports. It's to create a culture of continuous improvement where everyone is empowered to discover and reach their full potential. The most powerful AI analysis doesn't just tell us where we are. It illuminates paths toward where we could be.

In the next chapter, we'll move from analyzing data during implementation to evaluating outcomes, exploring how AI can help us assess effectiveness and make informed decisions about future directions. While analysis helps us understand what's happening in real time, evaluation helps us determine what worked, what didn't, and why.

EVALUATE

IN EDUCATION, EVALUATION SHAPES FUTURES. Students receive grades that determine college admissions and scholarship opportunities. Teachers undergo observations that influence career advancement. Schools receive ratings that affect funding and community support. Administrators face performance reviews that impact their professional trajectory.

These evaluations matter deeply, yet their implementation often falls short of their potential. Many students receive letter grades with minimal feedback about how to improve. Dedicated teachers participate in brief annual observations that barely scratch the surface of their classroom practice. Innovative schools see their unique strengths reduced to standardized metrics. Visionary administrators receive feedback that focuses more on management than leadership.

This isn't because educators don't value meaningful evaluation. I find it's quite the opposite. Teachers want to provide rich feedback that helps students grow. Administrators want to conduct observations that genuinely support teacher development. School leaders want evaluation systems that capture their schools' unique strengths and challenges. The challenge lies not in desire but in practical limitations of time, resources, and tools.

The good news is that we have the power to alter how educational evaluation can work. Artificial intelligence offers exciting possibilities to enhance evaluation processes, making them more meaningful, more personalized, and more actionable for everyone involved. Through the SAMR framework, we can progressively reimagine evaluation.

At the *substitution* level, AI can generate assessment supports and assist with observation notes, helping educators work more efficiently without changing the fundamental nature of evaluation.

At the *augmentation* level, AI enhances evaluation through improved grading systems and speaking skills assessment, adding capabilities that provide deeper insights with less administrative burden.

This chapter explores practical applications of AI-powered evaluation for students, teachers, and administrators. Rather than view evaluation as a necessary but limited process, the educational community can use these tools to create assessment systems that truly foster growth, improvement, and excellence.

You might notice that this chapter doesn't include examples at the modification level of SAMR. This is intentional and reflects an important distinction about evaluation itself.

The *modification* level of SAMR typically involves significantly redesigning tasks in ways that fundamentally change their nature. While we can substitute and augment how we evaluate, transforming evaluation into something entirely different would mean that it's no longer evaluation. Evaluation must maintain its fundamental purpose of determining what works, what doesn't, and why. If we modified evaluation to such a degree that it became something else entirely, we would lose the critical assessment function that education requires.

This doesn't mean AI can't change how we evaluate. It absolutely can, as we've seen through substitution and augmentation examples. We can make evaluation more efficient, more insightful, and more personalized while ensuring it remains anchored to its core purpose of measuring and understanding outcomes.

In the redefinition chapter, we'll explore how AI can help us move *beyond* traditional evaluation paradigms altogether—creating entirely new approaches to understanding educational effectiveness. But within the context of evaluation itself, our focus remains on enhancing and improving the assessment process rather than fundamentally changing what it means to evaluate.

I hope you'll see how AI can help fulfill evaluation's promise as a catalyst for improvement. We can take what is often a source of stress and transform it into an opportunity for meaningful development through specific, actionable insights rather than just summative judgments. In this way, we can make evaluations far more powerful tools for growth.

> AI optimism in evaluation means shifting from *assessment as judgment* to *assessment as insight*. When AI helps us evaluate more comprehensively, consistently, and efficiently, we can move learning forward through meaningful, growth-oriented feedback. The goal is to bring more responsive interactions to the evaluation system so educators can focus on individual needs.

SUBSTITUTION

Creating Assessment Supports

The first thing most teachers do for any assignment is write the directions. I don't know about you, but it always took me just a little extra energy to write directions that would be viewed in an LMS. I feel it's incredibly important for teachers to add great directions to the LMS or the top of the assignment page; it reminds learners what to do and provides clarity to people assisting the student outside of class. When I'm looking at my own children's assignments, I often see blank space where directions should be. If I ask my kids about the assignment, they'll say their teacher went over it in class. But there's no way for me to support them from home if I don't know what the teacher is expecting! So, using generative AI to write the assignment directions saves time and provides information for the student support system. This is a win for everyone.

You can start by dictating what you want learners to do into your go-to text or GPT tool. I find this simpler than typing it out because it will likely be exactly what I tell learners in class. Once you have the directions in text format, add a prompt.

> **SAMPLE PROMPT**
>
> These are the directions I gave to my ten-year-old learners. Rewrite the directions in a clear, concise format. Next, write three steps learners can take to complete the assignment. Then write two things learners can do to check for completeness.

Generative AI will give far more details than I would, and I can use this prompt over and over every time I make a new assignment! Make sure you check that the steps make sense and the completeness check fits the assignment, and then paste the results into your LMS or at the top of the assignment page.

Does anyone else remember RubiStar? I certainly used that website quite a bit during my first few years of teaching. RubiStar allowed me to quickly create rubrics with standardized formats, score criteria, and levels. I would copy and paste the content into Word, then modify the levels if needed. This was over twenty years ago, and the idea is the same today. AI rubric creation has received a few upgrades, though!

Use a GPT to create a rubric for an assignment by adding your assignment details, standards, and information like criteria and scale. Ask the GPT to create the rubric in the format that works best for you to copy and paste into another application. For example, if you're using Copilot, a table response will automatically give you the option to open it in Excel, while other tools might give you the option to download it as a PDF or Google Docs/Word document. Many apps now have the Common Core standards built in, so you can include them in the rubric instead of typing or pasting them into a prompt.

> **SAMPLE PROMPT**
>
> Create a rubric for me to assess my ten-year-old learners on their Minecraft build project. Their project should show originality of thought and clear communication, and it should meet the standards for history. Learners should have built a scene from a specific time period and labeled the scene appropriately. Use standards RL4.7, W4.7, W4.9, SL4.1, and SL4.4. Make the rubric in table format so I can export it. The rubric should have four levels. Use categories that include the standards as well as the project requirements.

Of course, you should adjust the rubric as needed to fit your requirements. I sent this prompt five times in two different GPTs, and I got completely different results each time. Consider regenerating responses and using the results that best fit your needs. Change your prompt as needed to create results that are closer to your goal. If you're using an app with a rubric generator, be sure to give clear directions and select the standards. Then don't be afraid of regenerating results the same way you would with a GPT. Remember that apps are using the same models any GPT is using, so they're not "better." But they're able to set clear parameters on your behalf, so sometimes you might get better results.

How else can you use AI to support assessment?

AI can generate hints for questions. Imagine giving learners a scaffolded opportunity to learn from a quiz. Give a GPT the questions and ask it to write a hint for each. Then add those hints to your favorite quiz tool as question feedback for incorrect answers. Allow learners to retake the questions (or the quiz as a whole). This makes the quiz more interactive and allows you to personalize the experience for each student. You could write the question hints yourself, but, now, generative AI can do it for you.

> **SAMPLE PROMPT**
>
> Here are five quiz questions for my world history class. Write a hint for each question to help guide learners to the correct answer. The hint should give learners direction without giving away the final answer.

Another assessment support is to create a bank of feedback to use with your learners. Often, teachers find themselves writing similar feedback over and over. I know many who save documents or spreadsheets for this purpose. They copy and paste the feedback into a response system as appropriate to the student work. Coming up with the responses is time-consuming, and deep thinking and creativity are needed to keep feedback from sounding canned. Utilize a GPT to come up with responses you can repurpose in your student assignments and ask for creativity! Include a pun about the topic, for example.

> **SAMPLE PROMPT**
>
> My fourteen-year-old learners are writing an essay about the journey of the hero after reading *The Odyssey*. I am assessing their writing based on the six traits of writing. I will likely use some of the same comments often. Please write three comments for each trait of writing. There should be one positive comment, one neutral comment, and one suggestion for improvement for each trait. When possible, include a pun, reference, or metaphor relating to *The Odyssey* in the comments.

Finally, as you've probably already figured out, you can also ask generative AI to assess student work on your behalf. This is substitution work, as you save time but have no other functional improvement (and likely lose a lot of knowledge about your learners). I will suggest in another chapter how you can use features in different apps to gain insights about your students' work through AI-powered tools. But for now, you can simply add the student work to a GPT or app, then ask the tool to generate feedback for the student. I have some words of caution about this practice, however. First, you must consider student privacy. If you're using a GPT or an app that stores your chat data, you are submitting your learners' intellectual property to a data set—potentially without their consent. There are legal implications to this practice. Second, you must consider bias and fabrications. Double-check the feedback before sending it to learners. Generative AI favors and produces a narrow range of text patterns based on its training. A student with a unique voice or informal English may not receive positive feedback from a tool because it doesn't understand the student's atypical strengths the way you do. Generative AI may also give feedback that simply doesn't match the work due to hallucinations. This will cause confusion for learners—and parents—if not checked.

> Every educator who thoughtfully incorporates AI into their practice is helping to shape the future of education. Your explorations, successes, and even occasional setbacks add insights to a profession that has always evolved through the courage of its practitioners.

Observing, Evaluating, and Modeling

School leaders are in a unique position to observe their staff using the proper tools, evaluating their use, and modeling what is best practice. In the case of generative AI, it is critical that leaders *lead* in this space. Use the tools, encourage teachers to use them responsibly, and model their use. I suggest specifically noting where and how you've used generative AI—you might even give staff insight into the prompt you used. This helps build capacity for prompt engineering in your school and gives teachers permission to use the tools for their own work. Ultimately, you are largely responsible for setting the tone for generative AI's adoption in your school. You can choose to embrace and innovate—or not. Begin substituting small tasks first. Get coaching on an email or the welcome message for back-to-school night. When you see or hear of teachers doing great things with generative AI, celebrate those wins. Of course, always follow your school and system policies on how these tools are to be used.

AUGMENTATION

Grading and Assessment

Imagine you've just given a multiple-choice and fill-in-the-blank test to your learners. Instead of manually grading each response, you use an AI-powered grading tool. Within minutes, the tool processes the answers, grades each test, and provides feedback to your learners. This feedback includes not only the correct answers *but also explanations for any mistakes*, helping learners understand where they went wrong and how to improve.

AI-powered grading tools exemplify the augmentation level by taking over the task of grading, which traditionally requires significant time and effort from educators. The functional improvement here is the speed and accuracy of grading, along with the ability to provide instant, detailed feedback to learners.

By automating the grading process, educators can reclaim valuable time that can be redirected toward more personalized teaching activities, such as one-to-one student support or lesson planning. Learners receive instant, detailed, and prescriptive feedback. This helps them quickly identify and address their mistakes, which can lead to better retention and understanding of the material.

There is an argument that AI grading tools ensure all learners are graded consistently and fairly. There isn't room for an educator to score an assignment based on their feelings about a particular learner or the context of an assignment. AI grading can reduce potential biases that might occur with manual grading. But it can also generate new bias: Remember that AI analysis favors native English-language writers who use more formal vernacular. I do not recommend using AI detectors for this and many other reasons.

AI grading tools can provide teachers with detailed analytics on learner performance, highlighting common areas of difficulty and allowing for targeted interventions. I remember teaching early readers and spending hours per week analyzing their daily work, then providing each student with a customized set of materials for the following week based on their data. It was incredibly time-consuming! With grading and analyzing data handled by AI, educators can finally focus on more creative aspects of teaching.

Try using a tool like Curipod or Writable to analyze and provide feedback on learners' written work. Check out ASSISTments or Microsoft's Math Progress to show learners corrections based on their missteps in math. Another tool is Gibbly, which is a gamified quiz creator. I love that Gibbly gives learners an opportunity to participate in the lesson!

Speaking Skills

Thanks to natural language processing and the advanced algorithms and massive data sets that come with large language models, we have some great ways for learners to practice their speaking skills independently, whether for a presentation or to practice a new language. Students previously depended on rehearsing in front of peers, families, or mentors to get feedback on their presentation skills. Now they have the tools available to rehearse and receive feedback on their own—so they don't have to be in front of a real audience before they feel ready. These tools also give *every* learner this support, no matter what access they have to help outside of school. I call that a functional improvement!

AI tools can use speech recognition technology to provide real-time, personalized feedback on various aspects of spoken language, including pronunciation, fluency, grammar, and vocabulary. For instance, if a learner mispronounces a word, the AI can highlight the error and offer suggestions for correction. This immediate feedback helps learners practice and refine their pronunciation, leading to more fluent and accurate speech. AI-generated feedback can also address grammatical errors and suggest more appropriate vocabulary. This helps learners enhance their language skills and become more confident speakers. If a learner uses incorrect verb tense, the AI can point out the mistake and provide the correct form. Plus, AI tools often catch errors that humans might miss. This is perfect for language learners since a large part of the learning is pronunciation, and that can't be supported through a textbook or even by watching a video. Many language learning apps have AI listening and feedback built in. SmallTalk2Me is one tool that is specifically designed for language learner interactions.

A full AI-supported process for learners to prepare for a presentation might look like this:

1. Learner uses generative AI to outline the speaker notes.
2. Learner uses dictation to talk about their knowledge of each point on the outline, capturing their speech for each point.
3. Learner prompts generative AI to revise their speaking based on a specific set of requirements for the assignment.
4. Learner rehearses with the revised content and makes adjustments to keep the presentation in their own natural style and tone.
5. Learner finalizes the speaker notes and begins practicing with an AI listening tool.
6. Learner adjusts their presentation style, body language, and pronunciation based on AI-generated feedback.

When learners are preparing for presentations, AI tools can analyze their speech for clarity, coherence, and engagement. The AI can provide tips on how to structure their presentation and maintain audience interest, and it can even gauge how effective their body language is (with video enabled). Learners can work on weaknesses and build on strengths without judgment, using the comprehensive feedback to develop strong presentation skills and perform better in public speaking scenarios. Microsoft's Speaker Coach is freely available for schools and is built into PowerPoint and Teams meetings. Learners and educators alike can launch Speaker Coach inside PowerPoint to receive personalized feedback anytime. Educators can also assign learner practice sessions and see the results through Speaker Progress. This is yet another functional improvement. As an educator, I can assign all my learners a practice session, then view the analytics from their rehearsal and work with small groups or individuals who need the most support. This process would have taken me weeks to complete by watching each learner's practice session!

Performance Analysis

Performance analysis in education involves systematically examining data to understand how individuals are progressing toward goals. With AI-powered tools, this analysis becomes more nuanced and can potentially reveal patterns and insights that might otherwise remain hidden.

AI can enhance how students understand their own progress as they shift from being passive recipients of grades to active participants in their learning journey. Digital portfolios with AI analysis features allow students to track their growth over time, identifying patterns in their work that might not be obvious through traditional assessment methods. This can be empowering for students in a class culture that promotes growth mindset and process over product.

For example, a high school student using an AI-powered writing platform might receive an analysis showing that while her argumentative essays are strong in evidence selection, she consistently struggles with counterarguments. The AI highlights specific examples across multiple assignments, providing a longitudinal view that a single graded paper couldn't offer. This concrete feedback empowers her to focus her efforts precisely where they'll have the greatest impact. A teacher may aim to recognize this specific information about each student, but the reality of an educator's caseload is a limiting factor beyond their control.

Middle school math students using adaptive learning platforms can access dashboards showing not just what problems they got right or wrong but what their misconception patterns are. Instead of seeing they got 70 percent correct on a fractions unit, a student might learn that they consistently make errors when the denominators are different but excel when working with equivalent fractions. This specificity turns vague awareness ("I'm not great at fractions") into actionable insight ("I need to practice comparing fractions with different denominators").

The most effective AI-powered self-evaluation tools don't just analyze past performance. They will also connect analysis to future action. When a student reviews their performance data, the AI might suggest specific practice activities, resources, or approaches based on their individual needs. The analysis-to-support connection in evaluative AI tools is exciting!

For teachers, AI performance analysis tools offer efficiency and depth that manual assessment approaches can't match. Rather than spend hours poring over individual assignments looking for patterns, teachers can use AI to quickly identify trends across classes, assignment types, and time periods.

When I taught middle school English, I had to review a set of ninety essays (three periods of students) every single week. Obviously, that was hours of my weekend, and I struggled to maintain consistency and track common issues across all papers. With AI assistance, I can still read each essay, but the AI can pre-analyze them and help me identify common strengths and challenges. I'm not recommending the AI evaluation tool replace the human review; it cannot and should not. But it can amplify data, provide insight, and identify patterns that would be difficult to quantify manually.

Beyond pattern recognition, AI tools can help teachers evaluate the alignment between their assessments and their instructional goals. A high school biology teacher might upload their unit test to an AI analysis tool that evaluates whether questions assess the intended standards and thinking skills. Perhaps most powerfully, AI performance analysis helps teachers identify unexpected correlations that might inform instructional decisions.

School leaders face the challenging task of evaluating teacher effectiveness across diverse classrooms, content areas, and teaching styles. AI-powered analysis tools help make this process more systematic and insightful. Rather than rely solely on infrequent classroom observations, principals can use AI to analyze multiple data sources over time. For instance, a school leader might combine observation notes, student performance data, and teacher-created assessments in an AI platform that identifies patterns in instructional effectiveness. The system might recognize that a particular teacher consistently excels at designing higher-order thinking questions but struggles with providing differentiated instruction for diverse learners.

AI can also help leaders identify successful teaching practices that might otherwise go unnoticed. By analyzing data from multiple classrooms, a tool might discover that teachers who implement specific discussion techniques show consistently higher student engagement and achievement across different subject areas. This insight allows leaders to highlight and share these effective practices more broadly. Wouldn't it be great if we could all benefit from our colleagues' expertise that might otherwise get missed?

For district-level administrators, AI performance analysis tools can reveal system-wide patterns that inform professional development and resource allocation. If data shows that teachers across multiple schools struggle with effectively teaching a particular mathematics concept, the district might prioritize specialized training in that area. Similarly, if analysis reveals that certain schools show consistently stronger results with similar student populations, leaders can investigate the practices contributing to that success.

Of course, some educators might feel concerned about the use of AI to evaluate data and make decisions about funding, resources, and staffing. Data has been used as a weapon against education too many times. We cannot let the poor decisions of some impact the good possibilities. The most effective use of AI for performance analysis in education maintains human judgment at the center while leveraging technology to provide richer, more nuanced information. The goal isn't to reduce evaluation to algorithms but to enhance human decision-making with insights that might otherwise remain hidden in the complexity of educational data.

Progress Monitoring

Progress monitoring tracks student learning and development over time. With AI enhancement, what was once a labor-intensive task requiring extensive manual data collection and analysis has evolved into a more dynamic, responsive, and insightful practice.

Traditional progress monitoring often involves periodic benchmarking in which educators test students at set intervals to measure growth. While valuable, this approach creates significant gaps between measurement points during which students might fall behind without detection. AI-powered tools solve some of these problems by enabling continuous, real-time progress tracking.

In elementary reading classrooms, tools like Storywizard and Microsoft's Reading Progress listen to students read aloud, automatically tracking fluency, accuracy, and comprehension. Rather than test reading levels quarterly, teachers receive ongoing data as students interact with texts, allowing for immediate adjustments to instruction. When a third grader suddenly struggles with multisyllabic words across several reading sessions, the teacher receives an alert suggesting targeted phonics intervention before the difficulty becomes entrenched.

Mathematics platforms like DreamBox and Zearn similarly monitor student progress as they work through problems, identifying not just correct or incorrect answers but the specific strategies students employ. This process-focused monitoring provides insight into students' mathematical thinking, revealing misconceptions that might be masked by correct answers or highlighting effective reasoning despite computational errors.

One of the most exciting aspects of AI-enhanced progress monitoring is its predictive capability. By analyzing patterns in student performance data, AI tools can identify early warning signs of potential academic challenges before they become serious problems. In Tacoma Public Schools, district leadership has been using predictive analytics and AI-powered bots for years to surface students most in need. Administrators quite literally receive an alert to their mobile devices to meet with a student whose data shows early warnings of risk. Their in-house early warning system monitors attendance, behavior, and performance—the top three categories that research shows strongly predict dropout risk. When the system flags a student who has missed several assignments in different classes (making it not immediately obvious) and the student is marked tardy a few days in a row, the counseling team can intervene with targeted support rather than wait for the student to fail.

In college settings, platforms like Georgia State University's GPS Advising use AI to track over eight hundred risk factors for every student. When a student registers for a course that doesn't align with their major requirements or shows a pattern of struggling with similar courses, advisers receive alerts enabling them to reach out proactively. This system has helped close achievement gaps and significantly increased graduation rates.

AI-powered progress monitoring doesn't just identify problems. It enables truly personalized learning pathways that adapt to each student's unique progress. Rather than move an entire class through a curriculum at the same pace, educators can use continuous progress data to customize learning experiences.

For students with IEPs, AI tools can track progress toward specific goals with unprecedented precision. A speech pathologist working with an elementary student might use an AI tool that analyzes speech samples during natural classroom interactions, providing detailed data on articulation improvement without requiring separate testing sessions. This naturalistic monitoring provides more authentic progress data while reducing time spent on formal assessment.

AI-enhanced progress monitoring also positively impacts how educational progress is communicated to students, families, and other stakeholders. Instead of waiting for report cards or parent-teacher conferences, everyone can access up-to-date information through user-friendly dashboards.

The evolution of progress monitoring through AI represents one of the most helpful enhancements in educational practice. By providing more frequent, detailed, and actionable information about student learning, educators can shift from reactive remediation to proactive support.

CONCLUSION

As we've explored throughout this chapter, artificial intelligence offers exciting possibilities to push educational evaluation into something more meaningful, insightful, and growth-oriented. By implementing AI evaluation tools across the SAMR framework, we can move beyond basic efficiency improvements to create assessment systems that provide the depth of feedback and actionable insights that students, teachers, and schools deserve.

The power of AI in evaluation lies in its ability to combine comprehensiveness with personalization. Traditional evaluation methods often force a difficult choice: Either conduct shallow assessments at scale or provide deep feedback to just a few. AI helps bridge this gap, making it possible to evaluate extensively while still attending to individual nuance and context.

For students, AI-powered evaluation means receiving specific, actionable feedback that illuminates not just what they got wrong but why—and how they might improve. It means assessments that adapt to their unique learning journey rather than enforce rigid timelines. Most importantly, it means evaluation that focuses on growth and mastery, helping students develop the metacognitive skills to assess their own work and direct their own learning.

For teachers, AI evaluation tools change the assessment process from a time-consuming obligation into a valuable source of insight about both student understanding and instructional effectiveness. By handling routine aspects of evaluation, AI frees educators to focus on the elements that most require human judgment, wisdom, and connection. Meanwhile, AI-enhanced classroom observations can provide more comprehensive, evidence-based feedback on teaching practice, creating richer opportunities for professional growth.

For administrators and school leaders, AI evaluation systems offer a more balanced understanding of institutional performance. Instead of relying heavily on standardized metrics, leaders can analyze patterns across multiple data sources, identifying both areas of excellence and opportunities for growth with greater precision. This more comprehensive evaluation approach enables more strategic improvement initiatives focused on what truly matters for student success.

Perhaps most significantly, AI-powered evaluation can help address the challenge of consistency and fairness. By reducing the impact of evaluator fatigue and time constraints, these tools help ensure that evaluations reflect actual performance and progress rather than circumstantial factors.

As you implement these evaluation approaches in your own context, remember that technology works best when it amplifies human strengths instead of attempting to replace them. The most effective AI evaluation systems combine technological capabilities with human wisdom, creating assessment processes that are simultaneously more insightful and more supportive of genuine growth.

In the next chapter, we'll explore how AI can support the ongoing management of educational processes, from scheduling and organization to policy development and discussion moderation. While evaluation helps us understand what worked and what didn't, management ensures that our systems run smoothly and efficiently.

MANAGE

BEHIND EVERY SUCCESSFUL LEARNING EXPERIENCE lies an intricate web of operations that most people never see. Meetings scheduled. Calendars coordinated. Policies drafted. Communications translated. Discussions moderated. Notes organized. Study plans developed.

These administrative tasks form the invisible infrastructure of education, consuming countless hours and creating friction that slows innovation. A counselor spends hours rescheduling meetings due to conflicts. A teacher struggles to communicate with parents who speak different languages. A student loses notes before an exam. An administrator labors for weeks developing a policy that other schools have already created.

These operational barriers don't just waste time. They directly impact educational outcomes by diverting attention from teaching and learning. Schools operate with limited resources and competing priorities, traditionally accepting administrative burden as an inevitable cost of educational service.

Artificial intelligence offers an alternative. By streamlining routine tasks, AI can remove friction from educational systems, handling operations with speed and accuracy. The result? More time for human connection, more energy for innovation, and ultimately more focus on what truly matters in education.

Through the SAMR framework, we can see how AI progressively changes operational management:

At the *substitution* level, AI handles basic operational tasks like meeting scheduling and translation, performing them more efficiently while maintaining their fundamental nature.

At the *augmentation* level, AI enhances operations through discussion moderation, note-taking, and personalized study plans that offer functional improvements beyond traditional approaches.

At the *modification* level, AI fundamentally changes administrative tasks through computer vision, policy development, and scheduling systems.

This chapter explores practical applications of AI-powered management for students, teachers, and administrators. While management aspects rarely make headlines, they impact daily experiences. A well-run school doesn't just accomplish goals more efficiently. It creates space for new possibilities that couldn't exist amid operational chaos.

When routine tasks no longer consume disproportionate time and energy, education professionals can redirect their focus to the aspects of their work that most require human creativity, judgment, and connection.

> The essence of AI optimism in management is recognizing that by removing operational challenges, we have room for educational innovation. Educators who have fewer administrative burdens can focus on the work that most directly impacts learning. The most powerful promise of AI isn't in doing old things more efficiently but in making new things possible by freeing human capacity for what matters most.

SUBSTITUTION

Meeting Scheduling

Finding meeting times can be quite a challenge for educators; teachers may have different free periods, other meetings may already be scheduled, or a necessary team member might be out sick for the week. So when I needed to schedule a meeting, I asked my tool to check my team's calendars and find a good time. Could I have done this with a scheduling assistant in Outlook? Absolutely. But it was a whole lot quicker to ask a digital assistant, and I had the added benefit of Copilot offering to set up the meeting on my behalf. This substitutes the time I would have spent checking calendars, creating a meeting request, and typing in all the details.

> **SAMPLE PROMPT**
>
> Suggest a time for our weekly team meeting when everyone is available. It should be scheduled before noon, early in the week.

For school administrators who coordinate dozens of meetings weekly with various stakeholders, this simple time-saving feature can reclaim hours that can be redirected toward more impactful leadership tasks. The real value isn't just in the minutes saved per meeting but in the cumulative effect of streamlining a task that occurs so frequently throughout the school year.

AI-powered meeting scheduling offers a straightforward substitution for the traditional manual process of finding available times and creating calendar invites. While the fundamental task remains unchanged, the efficiency gained allows educators and administrators to focus energy on preparing for productive discussions instead of coordinating when they'll occur.

AUGMENTATION

Discussion Moderation

One of the most common concerns I've heard from educators about online discussion forums is that learners will post inappropriate content. Educators often feel they need to moderate every post, which is unreasonable. Reading and monitoring every post in an ungraded discussion forum isn't reasonable either. While it's important to have adult oversight in class forums, AI can aid the educator here.

One of the critical roles of AI in online discussions is to flag inappropriate content. This includes identifying and addressing instances of bullying, harassment, or any language that violates the class's code of conduct. AI tools can scan for key words and phrases that are commonly associated with inappropriate behavior and alert the teacher or moderator. This allows for timely intervention, ensuring that the online learning environment remains safe and respectful for all participants.

AI monitoring tools can analyze the content of online discussions in real time, ensuring that conversations remain relevant to the topic at hand. These tools can identify when discussions veer off topic and gently nudge participants back on track. For example, if a discussion about a historical event starts to drift into unrelated personal anecdotes, the AI can prompt participants to refocus on the historical context. This helps maintain the educational value of the discussion and ensures that learning objectives are met.

Packback is a platform that provides AI-powered discussion moderation by automatically reviewing all student posts and flagging those that don't meet community guidelines. (It's also a writing coach.) If a student's post is flagged, they are notified and can make corrections to their post and republish to earn credit—without educator workload. Packback moderates posts containing plagiarism, profanity, logistic questions, and material it suspects is AI-generated, as well as low-depth and short posts. (I've already issued a warning about AI checkers, so remember that here.) By monitoring discussions, AI can provide insights into the quality of interactions. For instance, it can analyze the tone and sentiment of messages to identify when a discussion is becoming heated or unproductive. then suggest strategies to de-escalate the situation or encourage more constructive dialogue. Additionally, AI can highlight particularly insightful or valuable contributions, helping to recognize and reinforce positive participation. While deploying AI to monitor online discussions, it is imperative to ensure that these tools are used ethically and with respect for learners' privacy. Clear guidelines should be established about what the AI tool will monitor and how the data will be used.

Note-Taking

Voice-to-text technology supports note-taking by making the process more accessible and efficient. Learners can capture their thoughts and lesson content in real time, without the need to write everything down, meaning they can focus on understanding the material instead of worrying about the mechanics of writing. This reduces their cognitive load. Integrating voice-to-text technology into their study routines helps learners enhance their note-taking efficiency at home too. And such technology is particularly beneficial for learners with disabilities like dyslexia or fine-motor challenges, providing an alternative way to take notes and ensuring full participation in the learning process. Executive function supports like these make the difference between success and struggle for many learners.

Voice-to-text tools also support vocabulary and language skills as learners dictate their own notes. They can practice new vocabulary and more complex sentence structures without getting stuck behind a keyboard. Some advanced tools even offer real-time feedback, correcting errors and suggesting improvements as the learner speaks. This immediate feedback helps learners to refine their language skills over time and ensures that their notes are accurate and comprehensive.

Educators and learners should ensure that the tools they use comply with relevant privacy regulations and that their data is protected.

Microsoft OneNote is my favorite tool for note-taking, and it has dictation, audio, and transcription support built in. Learners can either record in a separate tool and upload to OneNote or record right from the page. Notes they take (either handwritten or typed) are timed to the recording during playback. Notes, audio, and transcription are all searchable, allowing learners to find information and sort their notes quickly.

AI-powered voice-to-text and transcription tools augment traditional note-taking by reducing the mechanical burden of writing while enhancing searchability, organization, and accessibility. This technology allows learners to focus more on understanding concepts than capturing them, creating a more efficient pathway to knowledge that particularly benefits those with learning differences or physical limitations.

Personalized Study Plans

A personalized study plan is a road map designed to help learners achieve their academic goals by considering their unique strengths, weaknesses, learning styles, and schedules. Unlike a generic study schedule, a personalized study plan adapts to the individual needs of each learner, ensuring that they focus on the right areas at the right times. The plan begins with an assessment of the learner's current knowledge and skills—especially in executive function. This helps identify areas of strength and areas that need improvement. Clear, achievable goals are set based on the learner's academic objectives. These goals can be short term (e.g., mastering a specific topic) or long term (e.g., preparing for a test). The study plan includes a schedule that fits the learner's daily routine, balancing study time with other commitments, ensuring that study sessions are spread out to avoid burnout and maximize retention. The plan identifies the best resources for each topic, such as textbooks, online courses, videos, and practice exercises, so that learners have access to high-quality materials tailored to their needs. The study plan is flexible and regularly reviewed to track progress and make necessary adjustments, helping the learner stay on track and continue to make progress toward their goals. Creating such a plan is labor intensive at best. Each learner needs guidance, modeling, and oversight to develop a plan that makes sense for their needs.

AI tools can quickly assess a learner's current knowledge and skills through quizzes and diagnostic tests. This helps identify strengths and weaknesses more accurately and efficiently than traditional methods. AI can help set realistic and achievable goals based on the learner's performance data and academic objectives. It can also generate a customized study schedule that fits the learner's availability and learning pace. AI can recommend the most effective resources for each topic, drawing from a vast database of educational materials. This ensures that learners have access to high-quality, relevant content. AI tools can monitor the learner's progress in real time, providing instant feedback and suggesting adjustments to the study plan as needed. This helps keep the learner on track and motivated. AI can create adaptive learning paths that adjust based on the learner's performance. If a learner is struggling with a particular topic, the AI can provide additional practice and resources to help them improve—without the learner feeling the judgment that comes with human interaction.

There are many AI tools that help learners create a personalized learning plan. A classic example, Khan Academy, begins by assessing a learner's current knowledge and skills. For instance, when preparing for the SAT, learners can take diagnostic tests that identify their strengths and weaknesses. This initial assessment helps tailor the study plan to focus on areas that need improvement. Based on the assessment results, Khan Academy generates a customized learning path for each student. This path includes specific lessons, practice exercises, and quizzes designed to address the learner's unique needs. Khan Academy's platform is adaptive. It adjusts the difficulty and type of content based on the learner's progress. This is the functional improvement that is core to Khan Academy's augmentation ability. As learners complete tasks, the system continuously updates their study plan to reflect their current understanding and performance. This guarantees that learners are always working on material that is appropriately challenging and relevant. They receive real-time feedback on their performance, helping them understand their mistakes and learn from them. The platform also tracks progress over time, allowing learners to see their improvement. The personalized study plans are flexible, based on learner schedule and pace.

Learners can also use GPT tools to create their own personalized study plans. Similar to the reflection prompts, educators can create a dedicated chatbot or provide learners with a prompt template.

> **SAMPLE PROMPT**
>
> I am fourteen years old and struggling with math. I need to create a personalized study plan to help me get back on track. I need to identify my strengths and weaknesses, learning styles, and schedule as well as my goals. Then I need to make a plan to include resources, study schedule, and a way to track progress. Act as my guidance counselor. Interview me to find out more information about me, then help me create a plan. Wait for me to respond to each question before continuing.

AI-generated personalized study plans augment traditional learning approaches by adapting to individual student needs, learning styles, and schedules in ways that static, one-size-fits-all plans cannot. These dynamic tools provide the scaffolding of a well-structured learning path while offering flexibility to adjust based on progress and performance, giving students greater agency in their educational journey while maintaining structure and guidance.

Translation

Translation technologies have evolved dramatically over the years, moving well beyond simple substitution into true augmentation of human communication capabilities. While basic word-for-word translation tools have been available for decades, today's AI-powered translation services offer functional improvements that allow us to connect across language barriers.

Modern translation tools don't replace human translators. (We still need real people connecting with other native speakers!) Modern tools, however, go beyond the possibilities of human translators to enhance communication in ways previously impossible. Consider the limitations of traditional translation: It typically goes one way, has a time delay, is limited to common languages, and lacks contextual understanding. AI-powered translation overcomes many of these constraints.

The school district where I worked served families speaking over 140 different languages. Hiring human translators for this diversity of languages would be both logistically challenging and prohibitively expensive. AI translation became not just a convenience but a necessity for equity and inclusion.

The augmentation value of today's translation tools comes from several key improvements:

> **REAL-TIME, MULTIDIRECTIONAL COMMUNICATION:** Unlike traditional one-to-one translation services, modern AI translation enables simultaneous, multidirectional communication. With Microsoft PowerPoint Live, Microsoft Teams meetings, and Microsoft Translator, the speaker presents in one language while each participant can choose their preferred language for captions and transcription. When speaking at a conference in Belgium in 2022, I presented in English while attendees simultaneously viewed captions. Some participants even selected French through

the PowerPoint Live session. This upgrades a formerly sequential process into a seamless, concurrent experience.

CONTEXTUAL UNDERSTANDING: Today's AI translation considers context, word order, cultural idioms, and even figures of speech. This is a significant functional improvement over literal word-for-word translation. This contextual awareness makes communication more natural and accurate.

ACCESSIBILITY ACROSS PLATFORMS: Translation capabilities are increasingly embedded within everyday communication tools, no longer requiring separate applications or services. This integration removes barriers to use and makes translation a natural part of digital communication.

SCALABLE PERSONALIZATION: Each participant can select their preferred language without affecting others' experience, which is a level of personalization that is completely impossible with traditional translation services or even with a room full of human translators.

Imagine a school's family night where every parent can participate fully, regardless of their primary language. As the principal speaks, each family member sees captions in their preferred language. Parents who couldn't attend can watch the recording later with the same translation capabilities through Microsoft Stream. These services bring inclusive, accessible communication to diverse school communities without additional costs or specialized equipment. Kathi Kersznowski and I wrote about this in our book, *Sail the 7 Cs with Microsoft Education*, because schools in our community were using Microsoft Translator to achieve amazing results by including more families in school events thanks to personalized translation tools.

I remain cautious about using generative AI models specifically for translation. While they might excel by incorporating regional expressions and cultural nuances, they could also perform poorly if they lack sufficient training data in certain languages or fabricate content that non-native speakers wouldn't recognize as incorrect. For critical communications, I still prefer dedicated translation services with proven accuracy.

The augmentation value of AI translation extends beyond efficiency. It creates entirely new possibilities for inclusive, multilingual environments where language differences no longer impede participation and understanding. This represents a functional improvement, allowing diverse communities to communicate, collaborate, and learn together.

MODIFICATION

Computer Vision

Computer vision tools can analyze images and generate detailed descriptions, helping learners build their vocabulary and improve their descriptive language skills. For example, an AI-powered image analysis tool can identify objects, actions, and settings in a picture, providing learners with rich, contextual vocabulary. This is particularly useful in language arts classes where students are learning to describe scenes, characters, and events.

Visual search tools allow learners to explore the world around them by taking pictures of objects and receiving instant information about them. Teaching new vocabulary in a real-world context like this makes learning more relevant and engaging. For instance, a learner can take or upload a picture of a plant or animal and learn its name, characteristics, and habitat. This is another nod to passion-based learning, in which learners choose what to focus on, then receive input for their interests.

These applications of computer vision align with various curriculum standards. For example, literacy standards often emphasize the importance of using descriptive language and acquiring new vocabulary through reading, writing, speaking, and listening activities. By integrating computer vision tools, educators can provide learners with interactive and immersive experiences that support these standards. Here are three tools that support computer vision:

GOOGLE LENS: This visual search tool allows learners to explore information about objects in their environment by simply taking a picture. It provides instant information and can be used to teach vocabulary and descriptive language in a real-world context.

GPTS: AI assistants can generate detailed descriptions of images, helping learners build their vocabulary and improve their descriptive language skills. Just upload a stored image, take a photo with your device, or link to an online image to get started.

SEEING AI: This groundbreaking free app developed by Microsoft is designed to assist the blind and low-vision community by narrating the world around them. It leverages the power of artificial intelligence to provide real-time descriptions of people, text, and objects through a smartphone camera. Users can benefit from the app's ability to read short text instantly; provide audio guidance to capture and read documents; identify products via barcode scanning; and recognize faces to estimate age, gender, and expressions. Additionally, Seeing AI can describe scenes, identify colors, read handwritten text, and even recognize currency notes. The app also includes indoor navigation capabilities and an audio-augmented reality experience for exploring unfamiliar environments. Seeing AI is a great tool for modeling what alternative text should be and how we use descriptive terms to create a mental picture for readers.

Let's consider how these types of tools are transformational. Learners can discover names, terms, descriptions, and additional information about things that are interesting to them. By self-selecting, learners use their own curiosity, modifying the task from learning what an educator has assigned to learning on their own. It reminds me of backward design. Instead of presenting the image as part of a lesson, or giving learners information and then asking them to find an image, these tools allow us to start with the imagery and work toward more information.

Learners can even take photos of themselves with Seeing AI and critique the automated description. Is it accurate? How would they describe themselves? How are these descriptive terms either encouraging or discouraging? What are the connotations of words like *old* or *thin*?

Of course, there are many more applications for computer vision in education: security, indoor mapping, parking management, vandalism prevention, facial emotion analysis, and attendance and crowd monitoring. Some of these applications are already in place at major public gathering spaces.

While computer vision technology offers many benefits, there are also challenges to consider. One potential issue is ensuring the accuracy and relevance of the information provided by AI tools. Educators need to verify that the content generated by these tools aligns with their learning objectives and curriculum standards. Another challenge is addressing potential biases in AI algorithms. For example, some AI tools may favor certain language patterns or cultural references, which could impact the inclusivity of the learning experience. Educators should be mindful of these biases and use AI tools as a supplement to traditional teaching methods, ensuring a balanced and equitable approach. Privacy and ethical considerations are also important when using computer vision tools. Educators should ensure that learners' data is protected and that the use of AI technology complies with relevant privacy regulations.

Mind Mapping

Another common activity in education is mind mapping. This could be called something else for you, but it consists of using a digital tool to organize ideas. We often add connections or categories to build or demonstrate understanding of concepts. Digital tools are usually a substitute for a physical ones like sticky notes, index cards, or poster paper. Many digital tools also add functional improvement, like the ability to sort, color, rearrange, store, search, and share information.

Here's one example. I asked Padlet's AI board creator to make a board of materials students might use in a makerspace. I removed the titles of the columns and replaced them with question marks. If I were introducing a group of learners to my makerspace in the school library, I might ask them to read through the materials and determine which categories fit each column. Then I would ask if they could think of any other materials we should add to the categories and which materials they might use for certain projects they have planned. It's a critical-thinking exercise as a jumping-off point for a lesson, changing the task from reading a list of materials to thinking about what they have in common.

Some organizing tools also have AI-powered options to sort the concepts instead of having the learners do it themselves. You might be thinking that it defeats the purpose of making a mind map if the learners don't have to find and make connections. But what if that's not the point? What if you, as the educator, created a set of terms that were not obviously related, then asked the AI to sort them? Next, ask learners to work independently or in groups to brainstorm how the ideas were sorted. What did the AI discover that these elements had in common? Is there more than one way to sort these ideas? (This reminds me of the Connections puzzle in the *New York Times*.)

Here is an example in Canva for Education. I made a list of sixteen terms having to do with airplanes, which supports the fourth-grade unit I teach on physical science, forces of motion, and flight. I selected all sixteen sticky notes and then selected to sort them by topic.

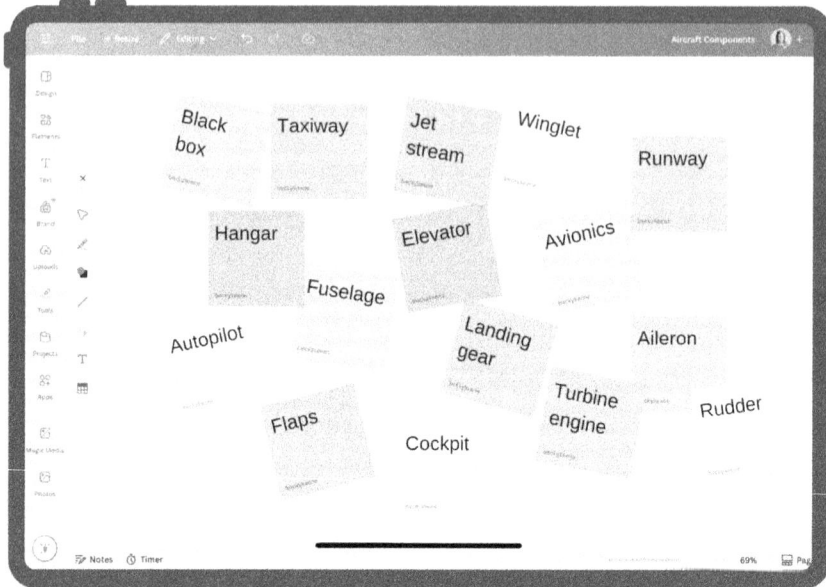

Canva rearranged the sticky notes and labeled them.

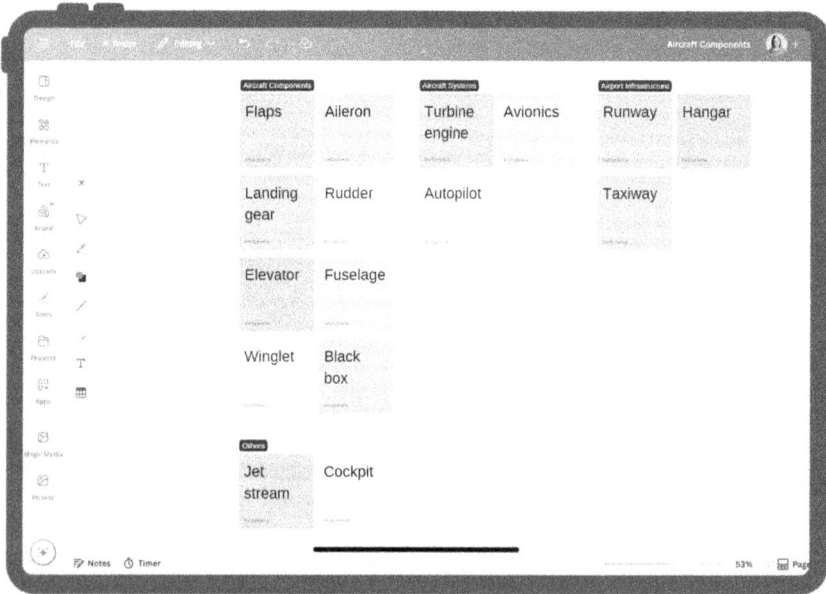

If I were going to use this activity with learners, I'd remove those category labels and ask them to figure it out! I could also give the students a template, let them ask Canva to sort the sticky notes into categories, and then host a discussion on whether they think things were sorted correctly.

Want to hear a little secret? When I was teaching eighth-grade humanities, my school district listed *The Odyssey* as required reading. Students went on to read *The Iliad* in ninth grade. I didn't feel like teaching *The Odyssey* to my eighth graders. I felt it was developmentally inappropriate, unengaging, and unnecessary. The high school teachers were expecting the students to show up with a basic knowledge of the text, though. So, I had my eighth graders read a summary of *The Odyssey* instead. We read about the characters, the themes, and the plot. I had the students design assessments for the district-wide question bank for the language arts department, including answer keys. By the end of the week, they knew *The Odyssey* shockingly well and were ready for their ninth-grade reading assignment.

While you might disagree with my deviation from the district-adopted curriculum, the fact is that my students knew all about *The Odyssey* without actually reading it, and that's another way we can use generative AI to support learners. Sometimes they need to know *about* a topic more than they need to have mastered it.

One last example is in FigJam. For this one, I asked FigJam's generative AI tool to create the mind map completely from scratch. I asked it to use themes and characters from *The Odyssey*. If I were using this now with learners, I'd ask them to research why these connections were made and what made them important. I would ask if there were better options based on their research, and then I'd ask them to defend one AI-generated response as more accurate than another. We might even use a debate prep tool (see the next section!).

Tools like Canva for Education and FigJam are subsets of much larger, enterprise-level companies and are currently free for education. Padlet has been in education a long time and has a subscription fee. Their AI-powered enhancements can be used to modify classroom assignments from traditional mind mapping to critical-thinking exercises that skip the dirty work (data entry) and move right into deeper thinking. Good stuff.

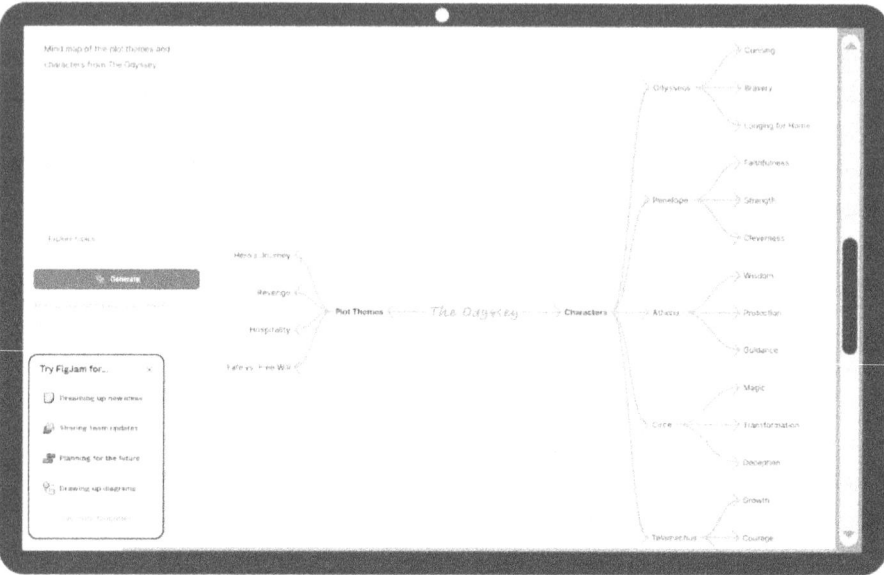

> The most important quality for navigating this AI journey isn't technical skill—it's resilience. When something doesn't work as expected, view it as data rather than failure. Each adjustment brings you closer to approaches that truly enhance learning for your unique context and students.

Policy Development

There has been so much discussion, collaboration, and concern around the world about creating policy for generative AI in schools—and rightly so! Several US states have released official guidance, and many school systems have published expectations, procedures, and more. Private organizations have posted public policy around generative AI. It would take a human many hours, if not days, to comb through this information without help. It would take a human even longer to summarize, synthesize, and analyze the data set for it to be useful and applicable in their own school system.

Fortunately, generative AI is great at all these tasks. The only issue for a human to consider is if the GPT contains the most recent information in its data set. Of course, this use case isn't dedicated to only artificial intelligence. Think about policies around athletics, attendance, behavior, grading, promotion, retention, academic integrity, extracurricular activities, staffing procedures, graduation requirements, and more. Prompt your favorite tool to create a summary of existing policies and provide information about loopholes, challenges, gaps, or concerns. Get ahead of potential issues in your own organization by asking AI to tell you what issues may lie ahead.

> **SAMPLE PROMPT**
>
> Find generative AI use policies from schools in Canada. First, compare the policies. Then summarize the themes present in these policies. Make a table of the themes with sourced examples for each theme. Finally, evaluate the policies for weaknesses. Write an analysis of how I can write a fair, responsible policy while considering the weaknesses.

Even though it's going to take up a lot of space here, I think it's important to share the output with you. Keep in mind this may not be correct, you may not agree with it, and it might not be current by the time you're reading this. But the output format and depth are what I want to demonstrate so you can see what's possible.

Comparative Analysis of Generative AI Use Policies in Canadian Schools

Summary of Policies:

1. Toronto District School Board (TDSB): Focuses on responsible and ethical AI use, integrating AI into the curriculum to enhance learning while addressing data privacy and academic integrity. Emphasizes teacher training and student awareness.

2. Vancouver School Board (VSB): Prioritizes safeguarding student data and privacy. Policies aim to balance innovation with caution, limiting AI use in high-stakes assessments while encouraging its use for personalized learning.

3. Calgary Board of Education (CBE): Advocates for the cautious integration of AI, stressing the importance of AI literacy among learners and staff. They highlight the need for continuous policy review and adaptation as AI technology evolves.

4. Ottawa-Carleton District School Board (OCDSB): Implements strict data privacy measures and provides comprehensive guidelines on acceptable AI use. Focuses on minimizing risks associated with AI, such as plagiarism and data security breaches.

Common Themes

Theme	Examples from Policies
Data Privacy and Security	VSB and OCDSB emphasize stringent data privacy measures to protect student information (Center for Democracy and Technology) (Site home page).
AI Literacy	CBE and TDSB stress the importance of AI literacy, including understanding AI's ethical implications and practical applications (Brookings) (D2L).
Academic Integrity	TDSB and OCDSB focus on preventing AI-related academic dishonesty, such as plagiarism, and provide clear guidelines on acceptable use (Digital Promise) (World Economic Forum).
Teacher Training	All districts highlight the need for ongoing professional development to help teachers effectively integrate AI into their classrooms (Brookings) (Site home page).
Responsible Use Guidelines	Policies from all districts include comprehensive guidelines on responsible AI use, aiming to create a safe and productive learning environment (D2L) (World Economic Forum).

Evaluation of Weaknesses

1. Lack of Consistency: Variations in policies across districts may lead to inconsistencies in AI use and understanding among learners and educators.

2. Rapid Technology Changes: AI technology evolves quickly, and policies may become outdated if not regularly reviewed and updated.

3. Resource Limitations: Effective implementation of AI literacy programs and teacher training requires significant resources, which might be a challenge for some districts.

4. Equity Concerns: Ensuring all learners have equal access to AI tools and education can be difficult, potentially widening the digital divide.

Recommendations for a Fair and Responsible AI Policy

1. Regular Policy Review: Establish a schedule for regular review and updates of AI policies to keep pace with technological advancements.

2. Centralized Guidelines with Local Adaptations: Develop centralized guidelines that can be adapted locally, ensuring consistency while allowing for contextual adjustments.

3. Comprehensive Training Programs: Invest in ongoing professional development for educators, ensuring they are equipped to integrate AI effectively into their teaching practices.

4. Focus on Equity: Implement measures to ensure all learners have equal access to AI tools and educational opportunities, such as providing necessary resources and support for disadvantaged learners.

5. Stakeholder Engagement: Involve a wide range of stakeholders, including educators, learners, parents, and AI experts, in the policy development process to address diverse perspectives and concerns.

> 6. Clear Ethical Guidelines: Define and communicate clear ethical guidelines for AI use, focusing on data privacy, academic integrity, and the responsible use of AI tools.
>
> By addressing these weaknesses and incorporating these recommendations, you can develop a fair and responsible AI policy that maximizes the benefits of generative AI while mitigating potential risks.

This example demonstrates how AI can rapidly synthesize information across multiple policies, identify patterns, and provide structured recommendations. For school leaders developing their own AI policies, this represents a significant time savings compared to manually researching and analyzing policies from other districts.

What's particularly valuable here is not just the summary of existing policies but the AI's ability to extract common themes, evaluate weaknesses, and generate recommendations based on this analysis. The task has changed from simple information gathering to insight generation, which provides leaders with actionable guidance for their own policy development.

However, this output also reveals some limitations. The AI appears to draw conclusions with confidence but without citing specific evidence for some of its claims. A school leader would still need to verify these findings against the original policy documents, particularly before making important decisions based on this analysis.

This is precisely where AI's "reasoning" or Think Deeper modes could significantly enhance the value of this output. With extended reasoning capabilities, the AI could do the following:

1. Provide more nuanced analysis of potential policy conflicts or implementation challenges
2. Explore the challenges faced in the space between innovation and privacy protection
3. Compare policy approaches against research on effective AI governance in educational settings

4. Evaluate policies through multiple ethical frameworks, considering diverse perspectives
5. Trace the potential consequences of different policy choices

For example, rather than simply recommend "regular policy review," a reasoning-enhanced analysis might identify specific triggers that should prompt reviews (like new research findings or technology developments) and suggest concrete ways to conduct those reviews effectively.

When working with AI for policy development and similar tasks, consider prompting the AI to engage in this deeper analysis explicitly. Ask it to reason through competing values, explore potential unintended consequences, or evaluate recommendations from multiple stakeholder perspectives. This approach uses AI as an information processor as well as a research partner. You can ask AI to analyze your own policy too. We've already covered how to get your documents into a GPT, but here's a reminder of two easy options:

- If your policy is on a publicly available website, use the Edge sidebar or a browser extension like Diffit or Brisk to "read" the content and respond with an output.
- If your policy is a PDF, upload the document to your generative AI app and prompt for information.

It's exciting to consider the possibilities of accelerating the creation or revision of school policy through the inputs of millions of other data points. In the past, schools have spent months interviewing other organizations and researching possibilities. While great attention and care should still be taken to draft and adopt a school policy, we can substitute generative AI into the research and ideation process and spend those saved minutes evaluating and personalizing the recommendations for our own schools.

> **SAMPLE PROMPT**
>
> Read this document. Compare it to other similar policies in your database. Then make a list of similarities and differences. Evaluate the efficacy of this document and provide feedback on how we can improve it.

Keep in mind that the outputs of prompts like these are designed to support the humans who are making big, impactful decisions. They are not meant to be copied and pasted and adopted! These outputs save decision-makers time by presenting them with self-service information that doesn't require outsourcing the process to a committee for a year. The benefits of moving into discussion and collaboration after synthesizing information quickly are considerable.

Scheduling

Creating an effective school schedule is important, cumbersome, and usually full of conflict. Everyone involved wants to focus on learning, education needs, and available resources. However, the process can be complex, involving a variety of challenging factors—especially with limited resources like educators and physical space.

AI-powered scheduling tools offer many benefits for schools. They automate the entire scheduling process, making it more efficient by considering all parameters and prioritizing factors such as room usage and educator availability. These tools are highly adaptable, allowing schedules to quickly adjust to unexpected changes like teacher absences or room reassignments. Additionally, AI can personalize schedules to meet individual learner needs and preferences, enhancing the overall learning experience. AI excels at resource optimization, so it can do a great job of allocating classrooms, equipment, and faculty time to ensure the best possible use of available resources. My recommendation is to create the parameters, then use AI to generate one or more drafts of schedules, and finalize the schedule with a human approach and several reality checks. Here's an example of this approach:

1. Define your requirements: Clearly outline the number of classes, teachers, learners, rooms, and parameters.
2. Select a tool: Select a versatile AI assistant like ChatGPT, Claude, Copilot, or a dedicated tool just for this purpose.
3. Input data: Provide the AI with all necessary scheduling details. Confirm you're using a data-protected environment if you're inputting anything personal or sensitive.
4. Generate and review: Use the AI tool to create the schedule and review it for any glaring issues.
5. Adjust: Make any necessary adjustments and export the final schedule in a suitable format like CSV.
6. Finalize: Fine-tune any remaining issues by hand.

> **SAMPLE PROMPT**
>
> Please create four school timetables for four classes of learners: freshmen, sophomores, juniors, and seniors. Each class should have the same daily schedule Monday through Friday. Use the following information for subjects and teachers. Advanced Math: Ms. Aisha Patel, Classroom 1; Literature: Mr. Carlos Martinez, Classroom 2; Modern History: Mrs. Mei Chen, Classroom 3; Chemistry: Dr. Ahmed Khan, Science Lab; Programming: Ms. Sofia Rossi, Computer Lab; Business Studies: Mr. Kwame Nkrumah, Classroom 4; Philosophy: Ms. Leila Hassan, Classroom 5; Art: Mr. Hiroshi Tanaka, Art Room; PE: Coach Maria Lopez, Gym; Biology: Dr. Fatima Al-Sayed, Biology Lab. Assume fifty-minute periods and a thirty-minute lunch break. School begins at 8:00 a.m. and ends at 3:00 p.m. Each class will take six periods of instruction plus one advisory period. Generate an example schedule.

Sample output:

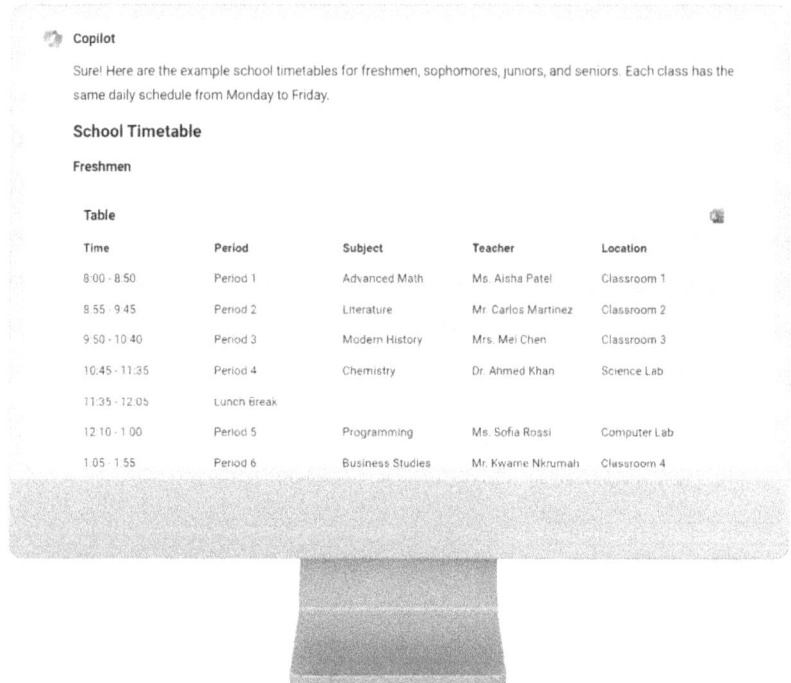

(The AI did give all four grade levels, but for sake of space, I've just included these first two.)

You might notice that Copilot assumed five-minute passing periods and adjusted the schedule to end at 2:50 p.m. based on the math.

You can use this same principle to create a master schedule for elementary specialists, reading group rotations, field day stations, year-long academic schedules like term and finals dates, holidays, and more. While someone at your school might miss a public holiday on next year's calendar, AI might not!

Administrative AI tools for scheduling can enhance equity by ensuring that operational decisions are made with consideration of their differential impacts on various student groups. AI scheduling systems can be designed to ensure that advanced courses remain accessible to all student populations or that teacher assignments don't inadvertently create tracks that limit opportunity.

These schedule creation tools also save time and can catch human errors. They can quickly and efficiently find a solution to small problems. It gives us something to work with without using a stack of sticky notes on a whiteboard, saving time for school administrators, counselors, and heads who have this task each year.

CONCLUSION

I hope you've been inspired by a glimpse into how artificial intelligence can improve the operational backbone of education. What emerges isn't just a more efficient version of traditional management (like we need another way to manage!). Instead, we can access a fundamentally different approach to running educational systems.

The impact of streamlined operations extends far beyond saving time, though that benefit alone is significant. When teachers spend less energy coordinating meetings and more time designing learning experiences, education improves. When students can organize their notes effortlessly and develop personalized study plans, learning deepens. When administrators can develop policies efficiently and moderate discussions effectively, leadership strengthens. These operational improvements create a cascading effect that touches every aspect of the educational experience.

For teachers, AI-powered management tools eliminate administrative friction that has traditionally consumed precious planning time. Meeting scheduling becomes effortless, multilingual communication happens seamlessly, and notes organize themselves automatically. These aren't merely conveniences. They represent the reclamation of professional capacity that can be redirected toward pedagogical innovation and student connection.

For students, these tools lead to greater independence and executive function. AI helps them develop personalized study plans, take more effective notes, and manage their learning materials. Skills like these extend far beyond the classroom! By removing logistic barriers to learning, AI management tools help students focus on content mastery rather than organizational challenges.

For administrators and school leaders, AI operations migrate from a constant struggle to a strategic advantage. Policy development becomes more efficient and data-informed. Scheduling optimizes limited resources. Computer vision enhances security and accessibility. Discussion moderation ensures productive communication. Together, these capabilities create educational environments where innovation can flourish because basic operations no longer consume disproportionate attention.

I'd also like to point out that AI-powered management creates equity of opportunity. When operational barriers fall, more educators and students can participate fully in the educational experience, regardless of their organizational skills or administrative support. A brilliant teacher with limited executive function can still create exceptional learning experiences. A student with organizational challenges can still demonstrate content mastery. A resource-constrained school can still operate with exceptional efficiency.

As you implement these management approaches in your own context, consider not just the individual tasks that might be improved but the systemic impact of smoother operations. When friction disappears from educational systems, new possibilities emerge, creative energy gets unlocked, and human connections previously limited by administrative burdens become possible.

In the next chapter, we'll move beyond the first three levels of the SAMR model to explore the transformative potential of redefinition. I'll cover AI applications that create entirely new educational possibilities that were previously inconceivable. While the management tools we've explored make existing systems work better, redefinition challenges us to imagine entirely new educational paradigms enabled by artificial intelligence.

PART III
REDEFINITION AND BEYOND

REDEFINITION

THIS CHAPTER WAS ALWAYS GOING to be different.

The thing about redefinition is that it changes the task completely. Unlike substitution, augmentation, or even modification, which enhance and improve existing tasks, redefinition fundamentally transforms the nature of the task itself. This level of integration allows for the creation of new, previously inconceivable tasks by leveraging technology to its fullest potential.

We've come a long way on our journey through SAMR and AI. We've designed learning experiences, created engaging content, supported diverse learners, analyzed data for insights, evaluated outcomes meaningfully, and managed operations efficiently. Each step has offered valuable improvements to education. But now we arrive at the threshold of something truly extraordinary.

Redefinition is where transformation happens. It's where constraints that have shaped education for centuries suddenly dissolve. It's where students and teachers discover possibilities that couldn't have existed before. It's certainly not because educators lacked imagination; it's because the tools simply weren't there. This is the realm of the previously impossible made accessible.

I remember the first time I witnessed true redefinition in action. A student who had always struggled with writing was using AI to rapidly generate story ideas, exploring different narrative paths and character developments with a freedom and fluidity that traditional writing methods never allowed. The smile on his face wasn't just about easier writing. It showed the joy of discovering creative possibilities he never knew he possessed. His relationship with storytelling had been fundamentally changed. He wasn't just doing the same task better; he was engaging with narrative in an entirely new way.

This is the promise of redefinition. Not merely improvement, but transformation. Not just efficiency, but reimagination. Not simply doing things better, but doing things we never dreamed possible.

> At the heart of AI optimism is the belief that we now have full access to educational possibilities that were previously impossible. Redefinition is about reimagining what education can be when we truly begin to use AI as a partner in creation instead of a tool for automation. The AI optimist sees beyond limitations to envision learning experiences that are more personalized, more creative, more equitable, and more deeply aligned with the uniquely human capabilities that will define success for students in their futures.

In previous chapters, we organized our exploration around educational processes: design, create, support, analyze, evaluate, and manage. But at the redefinition level, these categories begin to blur and blend. When students become designers of immersive learning experiences, when they collaborate with AI to create previously inconceivable works, when they analyze data in ways that reveal hidden patterns across disciplines, the traditional boundaries between educational roles and processes start to dissolve.

That's why this chapter takes a different approach. Here, we'll explore applications of AI that don't just enhance education. They reinvent it. We'll see examples of learning experiences where students aren't merely consumers of content but co-creators of knowledge. We'll discover assessment approaches that don't just measure learning but actively foster it. We'll examine learning environments that adapt not just to students' current abilities but to their unique potential.

The educational future that emerges at the redefinition level isn't just more efficient or engaging. It's also more human! By leveraging AI to handle tasks that machines do best, we create space for the deeply human aspects of learning: creativity, critical thinking, collaboration, and connection. Rather than diminish human capability, AI at the redefinition level amplifies it, creating new possibilities for expression, discovery, and growth.

Perhaps the best potential of AI lies in its ability to help us reimagine education systems that have historically sorted students into winners and losers along predictable demographic lines. At the redefinition level, AI enables us to create learning environments that truly adapt to and value the diverse strengths, backgrounds, and learning styles that students bring instead of demanding that they align to a narrowly defined notion of academic success.

As you explore this chapter, allow yourself to feel excited about these possibilities. Education has always been about unlocking human potential. With AI as our partner in this mission, we stand at the threshold of an educational renaissance where learning becomes more personalized, more creative, more meaningful, and more joyful than ever before.

Welcome to redefinition—where the future of education begins.

Let's start by looking at some examples of how we use generative AI for redefinition in our daily lives. Have you interacted with AI in any of these ways?

Content Creation and Writing

ORIGINAL TASK: Writing articles, blog posts, or marketing content manually.

REDEFINED TASK: Using AI-powered natural language apps to generate content. Writers focus on refining and personalizing the content, while AI handles the bulk of the initial drafting. This allows for more creative and strategic thinking rather than just the mechanics of writing. The task becomes editing instead of authorship.

When ChatGPT was first released, my daughter asked a profound question: "Which is more important, the author or the editor?" Worth thinking about!

Virtual Companions

ORIGINAL TASK: Traditional therapy sessions with human therapists attended live, synchronously.

REDEFINED TASK: AI-driven virtual companions provide emotional support and mental health check-ins throughout a day or week whenever the patterns suggest the human might need a mental health break. AI companions engage in conversations, offer coping strategies, and even detect early signs of mental health issues to report to a trusted adult. The task becomes personalized, customized wellness check-ins instead of human-initiated ones or live sessions.

AI-Generated Art Exhibitions

ORIGINAL TASK: Artists creating and displaying their work in galleries.

REDEFINED TASK: AI-generated art exhibitions where AI creates unique pieces of art based on various inputs and themes. Exhibition viewers focus on the prompts as well as the outcomes, helping them understand the process behind the art. AI-generated art may include themes and modalities (even three-dimensional ones), like location or culture, that are unique to the gallery's context. Exhibition viewers review how patterns in society impact the generated art.

AI-Powered Storytelling

ORIGINAL TASK: Authors writing novels and stories manually.

REDEFINED TASK: AI collaborates with authors to create interactive, branching narratives where readers can influence the storyline. This transforms the traditional reading experience into an interactive adventure, blending gaming elements with literature. The reader becomes a part of the story, generating content unique to them.

Personalized Music Composition

ORIGINAL TASK: Musicians composing and performing music.

REDEFINED TASK: AI generates personalized music tracks based on individual preferences and moods. Users can input their current feelings or desired atmosphere, and the AI composes a unique piece of music tailored specifically to them, creating a deeply personal and novel musical experience. Instead of requesting a particular artist or song, AI predicts emotion based on input data and generates appropriate vibes. The task for the human then becomes responding to the music selections with feedback to create personalized algorithms.

Now, I have to say, I realize AI-generated art is controversial! None of my writing is meant to undermine the power, creativity, or intellectual property of the human artist. My goal is to showcase the possibilities of an AI world.

At the heart of redefinition is empowering learners to become creators rather than consumers. This shift is the largest part of redefinition because it can create a deeper level of engagement and ownership over learning. When learners are given the tools and freedom to create, they are not just absorbing knowledge; they are actively constructing it. This process encourages critical-thinking and innovation skills that are essential for their futures. In the twenty-first-century learning design framework, the highest levels of collaboration, problem-solving, knowledge construction, and skilled communication often involve task redefinition.

For teachers and administrators, embracing redefinition means releasing some control and trusting learners to take the lead in their learning journeys. This can be a challenging transition, but it is necessary for developing an environment where learners can demonstrate their understanding in new and meaningful ways. By stepping back, educators allow learners to explore, experiment, and express their learning creatively. This might involve learners designing their own projects, using AI to create immersive learning experiences, or collaborating on global issues through digital platforms.

In a pre-AI school setting, redefined lessons often include learner choice, nontraditional tasks, and authentic audiences. Some of you might already be leading your students through amazing learning experiences like these. What does it look like to layer generative AI on top of these projects?

Elementary Learners: Virtual Field Trips with Interactive Elements

Imagine a third-grade class studying marine biology. Instead of reading about ocean life in textbooks, students embark on a virtual field trip to a coral reef. Using VR headsets, they explore the reef, interact with marine life, and collect data on different species. Back in the classroom, they use this data to create interactive digital presentations, complete with videos, images, and their own voice-overs explaining what they learned. This task redefines traditional learning by immersing students in an interactive environment and allowing them to present their findings in a dynamic, multimedia format.

Brainstorm: How would you use generative AI with students to support this project?

Middle School Learners: Collaborative Global Projects

In a seventh-grade social studies class, students collaborate with peers from a school in another country to tackle a global issue, such as climate change. Using digital collaboration tools, they conduct joint research, share findings, and develop a comprehensive action plan. They create a shared digital portfolio that includes videos, infographics, and written reports. This project redefines learning by nurturing international collaboration and enabling students to address real-world problems in a meaningful way.

Brainstorm: How could your students use generative AI along with you (in small groups or whole groups) to support their projects?

Secondary School Leaners: Prototype Designing and Building

High school students in a STEM class are tasked with designing and building prototypes to solve a community problem, such as creating a sustainable water filtration system. They use CAD software to design their prototypes, 3-D printers to create models, and sensors to test their effectiveness. Students document their process and results in a digital portfolio, which they present to local community leaders. This task redefines traditional assignments by integrating advanced technology and real-world problem-solving, giving students hands-on experience in engineering and design.

Brainstorm: How would these students use generative AI on their own to complete their work?

Redefinition opens a myriad of possibilities for learners to showcase their understanding. Instead of traditional tests and essays, students might create interactive simulations, develop AI-driven applications, or produce multimedia presentations that integrate various forms of technology. These new methods not only make learning more engaging but also provide a more comprehensive assessment of understanding and skills. Redefinition is about breaking down the barriers of traditional education and reimagining what learning can look like. It is about creating a dynamic, learner-centered environment where technology is not just a tool but a catalyst for innovation and creativity. I can't wait to jump into these ideas with you! But before we do, one last word of encouragement from the amazing Ethan Mollick, who writes this in his book *Co-Intelligence*: "Our new AIs have been trained on a huge amount of our cultural history and are using it to provide us with text and images in response to our queries. But there is no index or map to what they know or where they might be most helpful. Thus, we need people who have deep or broad knowledge of unusual fields to use AI in ways that others cannot, developing unexpected and valuable prompts and testing the limits of how they work."[2] I believe this includes you—and your learners!

---

2   Ethan Mollick, *Co-Intelligence: Living and Working with AI* (Portfolio, 2024).

PROMPT VOCABULARY

Reverse prompting is a great way to build vocabulary with learners. Instead of asking them to write prompts, define images, or learn new terms without context, have them use visual search or apps like Ideogram to get extended information.

First, try using an app that will accept image uploads. Ask the app to describe the image. I used a GPT and uploaded an image of the Wright brothers' first flight. Then I entered this prompt:

> **SAMPLE PROMPT**
>
> Describe this image in detail.

Response:

> This image shows a historic moment related to early aviation, specifically one of the Wright brothers' flights. The scene captures the Wright brothers' glider being carried by two men, likely Orville and Wilbur Wright, on a sandy surface that resembles the dunes at Kitty Hawk, North Carolina. The glider, a biplane, has a lightweight frame with two sets of wings stacked vertically. The structure is made of wooden beams and fabric

> that provide the lift. One of the Wright brothers is positioned prone in the center of the glider, lying on his stomach to operate it, while the other brother and an assistant are on either side of the glider, holding on to the aircraft's wingtips. The photograph is in black and white, indicating that it dates back to the early twentieth century, during the period of the Wright brothers' pioneering flights. The background is a clear sky with no clouds visible, emphasizing the aircraft and its operators. The setting is likely a remote and open area suitable for testing the early flying machine, emphasizing the experimental nature of early aviation endeavors.

If this was a reading activity, I'd be having you annotate this text. Look at all that vocabulary building! If you have multiple people try this together, you'll notice similarities and differences in the results. This is a great opportunity to infer definitions, determine synonyms, and understand connotations.

Next, try adding a vague input such as this to Ideogram for image generation: Draw a plant cell. Then leave Magic Prompt on and choose Create. Ideogram will generate four options for images to match your prompt, all with different extended prompts generated by AI. For my example, a plant cell, Ideogram generated four different results with four very different images:

> A plant cell with a central vacuole, chloroplasts, and a cell wall. The vacuole is large and takes up most of the cell. The chloroplasts are scattered throughout the cell. The cell wall is thick and rigid, giving shape to the cell. The cytoplasm is dense with ribosomes, mitochondria, and other organelles.

> A plant cell is a small compartment within the cytoplasm of a plant. Inside the plant cell is a large central vacuole, surrounded by a thin layer of cytoplasm. The vacuole is a storage compartment for water, nutrients, and waste products. The cell wall is a rigid layer outside the cell membrane, providing support

and protection. The cell wall is made of cellulose, a complex carbohydrate. There are also small, circular structures called chloroplasts, which are involved in photosynthesis.

A detailed illustration of a plant cell. The cell wall is brown, and the cell membrane is a thin, pink layer around the cell. Inside the cell, there's a large green chloroplast floating in the cytoplasm. There's also a small purple nucleus near the bottom of the cell.

A detailed illustration of a plant cell. The cell wall is shown as a thick, wavy line. Inside the cell, there is a large round nucleus with a few smaller structures. There are also a few vacuoles, mitochondria, and a large central vacuole. The background is a light blue gradient.

You can then edit these extended prompts for details and regenerate a more specific image. Just look at all the vocabulary embedded in this response.

REAL-WORLD DATA SETS

Using real-world data sets in education is important (and more engaging) because it makes learning more relevant through connecting classroom lessons to real-life scenarios, which can significantly increase student motivation and interest. Analyzing real-world data requires students to apply critical-thinking and problem-solving skills, helping them interpret data, identify patterns, and draw meaningful conclusions. I believe these are essential skills for the twenty-first century. Real-world data analysis often involves multiple disciplines, such as math, science, and social studies, supporting interdisciplinary understanding and helping students see the connections between different fields of study. In our data-driven world, the ability to analyze and interpret data is a future-ready skill. Possibly most important, access to real-world data empowers students to explore issues that matter to them, such as climate change or social justice, inspiring them to become informed and active citizens.

We used to be limited to the data in encyclopedias—outdated upon publication and at times difficult to find. In the internet age, data sets are publicly available on websites and curated through educational websites. In the age of AI, we can simply ask for what we want to find. If it's available on the internet, the algorithms will find it. I do highly recommend, as always, using an AI tool that cites its sources for this task. Then follow the links and double-check that AI isn't fabricating information. It's also helpful to use an internet-connected GPT so you're receiving the most recent data. Older data sets are limited to years past.

Here are examples of data sets that might get used in any classroom:

- **Climate analysis:** Learners analyze historical climate data to identify trends and make predictions about future climate patterns.
- **Economic data:** Learners use data from the World Bank to study economic indicators like GDP, unemployment rates, and inflation across different countries.
- **Health and well-being studies:** Learners examine data sets on public health issues, such as the spread of diseases or the impact of vaccination programs.
- **Social studies projects:** Learners analyze demographic data to study population growth, migration patterns, and urbanization.
- **Sports statistics:** Students use sports data to calculate player statistics, review team performance metrics, and predict game outcomes.
- **Music analysis:** Students explore data sets related to music, such as streaming statistics, genre popularity, or the impact of music on mood and productivity. For example, they might analyze how different genres affect study habits or how music trends have evolved over time.

- **Video game data:** Students use data from video games to study player behavior, game design, and the impact of gaming on cognitive skills. They could analyze data sets from platforms like Steam or specific games to understand player engagement and game mechanics.

Here's how different groups can use real-world data sets:

- **Teachers:** Before starting a unit, gather real-world data from reliable sources. Use this data in combination with Claude or Canva Sheets to create interactive graphs and charts for students to analyze.
- **Students:** Use video game data to study player behavior and game design. Gather data through AI prompting, then analyze it with AI to provide insights. Understand what makes certain games more popular and how game mechanics influence player engagement and behavior. This can be tied into lessons on statistics, psychology, and even computer science.
- **Administrators:** Use public health data to assess the effectiveness of school health programs. For example, analyze vaccination rates and the incidence of preventable diseases within the school community. This data can inform decisions about health initiatives and resource allocation, ensuring that the school is effectively addressing student health needs.

ASSESSMENT SWAP

Have you ever wished you were a fly on the wall during a conversation? Many AI tools give teachers and administrators oversight of student chats with AI apps and assistants. Many AI tools also enable sharing the chat history for a single conversation. Just select the Share button wherever you see it inside a chat. This creates a publicly accessible link that can be copied and pasted into an email, chat message, website, newsletter, assignment, and anywhere else you can paste text. That's great news because viewing the thinking and prompting behind another human's inputs can be incredibly valuable for several reasons.

First, it provides insight into the person's cognitive processes, revealing how they approach problem-solving and critical-thinking tasks. This transparency allows educators to identify specific areas where a learner may struggle or excel, enabling more targeted and effective support. Additionally, understanding the prompts and questions that guide a learner's thinking can help educators refine their instructional strategies, ensuring they are asking the right questions to stimulate deeper learning. For all ages of learners, reflecting on their own thought processes can advance metacognitive skills, helping them become more aware of how they learn and how to improve their strategies. Focusing on the process over the product promotes a more personalized understanding of learning and growth.

PROMPTATHONS AND PROMPT LIBRARIES

A promptathon or prompt library activity focuses on a single prompt (or set of prompts) as the outcome. These innovative activities engage students and educators in the creation and refinement of prompts used for AI interactions. In a promptathon, participants work together to brainstorm, test, and improve prompts, often in a competitive or collaborative setting. This process encourages creativity, critical thinking, and iterative improvement as participants see how different prompts yield varied responses from AI tools. There might even be awards given at a promptathon! It's practically an esport.

In a less competitive event, participants combine their best prompts into a prompt library. Collaborative prompt libraries are the collective curation of effective prompts that can be shared and utilized across people and groups. Prompt libraries can become valuable resources for learners, educators, or administrators looking to enhance their prompt strategies and serve as inspiration for individual AI interactions.

The value of these activities lies in their ability to cultivate a deeper understanding of how AI tools can be leveraged for learning. By focusing on the creation and refinement of prompts, students and educators gain insights into the mechanics of AI, including how language and context influence AI responses. This hands-on experience can demystify AI technology (it's not magic, after all) and empower participants to use AI more effectively. Additionally, these activities promote collaboration and knowledge sharing, as participants learn from each others' successes and challenges. This collaborative spirit not only enhances the quality of the prompts but also builds a sense of community and shared purpose among participants.

Promptathons and prompt library activities redefine learning by shifting the focus from one final product to the input at the start of a task. Instead of consuming information by taking a quiz on how to prompt AI, students become active creators and evaluators of content that holds value for an authentic audience—either competition judges, their peers, or other users. This approach is a more inquiry-based learning environment, where participants are motivated to experiment, iterate, and reflect on their learning processes.

MICROCREDENTIALS

Another interesting use case for redefining learning tasks through AI is microcredentials and badges. Awarding AI badges for exemplary skills can be a great way to recognize and motivate learners, teachers, and administrators. This is also a way to align learner goals with future-ready skills. These badges can serve as a tangible recognition of skills and achievements, encouraging continuous learning and excellence in AI use across the school community.

Ensuring that AI badges are fair and unbiased involves several key strategies. First, establish transparent and objective criteria for awarding badges, clearly defining the specific skills, behaviors, and achievements required for each badge. Give students access to their performance data and make sure they understand the rationale behind badge awards—and that they can challenge decisions they perceive as unfair. This transparency builds trust and helps all participants understand the expectations and work toward their goals.

Additionally, use a diverse group of evaluators, including teachers, peers, and unbiased AI tools, to help identify and mitigate biases and provide a balanced perspective. Regularly review and update the criteria and processes for awarding badges, incorporating feedback from learners, teachers, and administrators. And remember, it's important to ensure AI tools used in evaluation are designed and tested to be free from biases, using diverse training data and regular fairness audits.

Also, design badge criteria and evaluation processes to be inclusive of all students, regardless of their background or abilities. This includes considering different learning styles, providing necessary accommodations, and ensuring equal opportunities for all students to earn badges.

Here are some potential categories for AI microcredentials:

TEACHERS:

- **Curriculum design:** Develops lesson plans that effectively incorporate AI tools
- **Assessment:** Creates and implements assessments using AI tools
- **Professional development:** Completes advanced training or courses in AI education
- **Innovation:** Demonstrates innovative uses of AI to enhance teaching and learning
- **Mentorship:** Guides and mentors students in their use of AI tools
- **Data-driven decisions:** Uses AI to analyze student data and inform instructional strategies

- **Ethics and safety:** Promotes and ensures ethical and safe use of AI in the classroom

STUDENTS:

- **Literacy:** Demonstrates a strong understanding of basic AI concepts and terminology
- **Creativity:** Crafts innovative and effective prompts for AI tools
- **Ethics:** Understands and applies ethical considerations in AI interactions
- **Collaboration:** Successfully collaborates with peers using AI tools for group projects
- **Problem-solving:** Uses AI to solve complex problems or complete challenging tasks
- **Integration:** Effectively integrates AI tools into class projects or assignments
- **Research:** Utilizes AI to conduct thorough and insightful research

ADMINISTRATORS:

- **Leadership:** Leads initiatives to integrate AI across the school or district
- **Policy development:** Creates policies that support ethical and effective AI use
- **Professional development programs:** Organizes and facilitates AI training for staff
- **Resource management:** Efficiently manages AI tools and resources within the school
- **Data-driven decision-making:** Uses AI-analyzed data to make informed administrative decisions
- **Community engagement:** Promotes AI literacy and engagement within the school community

- **Innovation:** Implements innovative AI projects or programs that benefit the school

PHYSICAL SPACE CONSTRUCTION

AI-powered physical space construction in virtual environments is revolutionizing the way we design and interact with educational spaces. By leveraging AI tools, anyone can become an architect who creates detailed and immersive simulations of schools, classrooms, playgrounds, libraries, and other spaces. This technology allows for a more collaborative and iterative design process, where everyone can visualize and modify spaces in real time, ensuring that the final design meets the needs and preferences of the people who will be accessing it. It's design thinking at its best! Additionally, these virtual environments can be used to test different layouts and configurations, optimizing the use of space and resources before any physical construction begins. What if teachers used a physical construction tool to redesign their classroom with the input of the students who will be using the space?

Any image generator that allows reference images can help you get started. Just take a photo of the physical space, upload your reference images, and ask ChatGPT to create a mock up with your ideas.

See a TikTalkWalk about this here!

> **SAMPLE PROMPT**
>
> Use this image of my classroom as a reference. Help me visualize a new arrangement. Add a teacher's desk, reading chair, fiddle leaf plant, and bookshelf.

Promethean AI is one tool that supports physical space construction by enabling educators, students, and administrators to create detailed and immersive virtual environments. It automates the creation of 3-D environments, using AI to generate detailed and diverse game worlds based on simple descriptions so users can design and visualize spaces without designing from scratch. The platform supports a wide array of environment types and offers a natural language interface for easy interaction, making it accessible for learners.

CURIOSITY COACHING

Besides just being an interesting name for a thought process, curiosity coaching is a really cool approach to learning. It's a little constructivist, a little Montessori, and a lot motivating. Curiosity coaching uses AI to guide humans through a personalized journey of exploration and discovery. Imagine a student who has just finished a lesson on photosynthesis and is wondering why some plants have different leaf colors. He opens his AI assistant and asks this question, which leads him to learn about pigments like chlorophyll and anthocyanins. As he continues, the app generates an illustrated concept map of his learning path and suggests new directions to explore. The app suggests follow-up learning through questions at the end of each response. Eventually, the learner finds himself discovering more about the effects of light wavelengths on plant growth and the role of photosynthesis in different ecosystems, connecting with a previous exploration about the Amazon rainforest. This self- and AI-driven learning journey not only satisfies his immediate curiosity but also deepens his understanding and links separate topics in a meaningful way.

In the traditional K–12 setting, students often have limited opportunities to explore their interests beyond the prescribed curriculum. Occasionally, an educator might notice a learner's curiosity and suggest additional resources, but AI tools can take this further. With their excellent memory and ability to generate relevant prompts, tools like Hello Wonder, Curio, and Moxie can continuously engage students in their learning journeys. These tools can act as curiosity coaches, providing safe and creative environments for young learners to explore. Early attempts at true curiosity coaching, such as SocratiQ, show promise by combining elements of interactive platforms like Miro and Wikipedia. Mindjoy focuses on building chatbots to respond in ways that impact learner curiosity. These tools can also enhance social connections, linking learners with peers who share similar interests and potentially sparking long-term passions and projects.

TEAM COACHING

Speaking of coaching . . . group project coaching, or team coaching, is yet another way AI can support education in a transformative way. Many learners dread group projects, and we all know how poorly they can go if learners aren't all invested in the process and product. Educators often spend much of their class time coaching learner groups. Likewise, not all adult teams are highly functional either. Often there are barriers to productivity, whether it's a lack of executive function or a lack of team unity. Without mentorship, groups can become dysfunctional and unproductive. Ultimately, participants can be frustrated and the project results are unsuccessful.

AI can significantly enhance the process of coaching group projects by providing tools that facilitate collaboration, organization, and personalized feedback. This helps redefine the first-order task from facilitating group work to actually doing the work. Explore tools like Trello with Butler, Miro, and Slack to create an AI-empowered group collaboration space.

CAREER EXPLORATION

Earlier, I wrote about how administrators could use generative AI apps to create bots to assist learners with career counseling. That's a great starting point, and it's easily accessible for any school. However, schools can choose to level up the career exploration experience for learners with AI tools that provide an opportunity to test out a career inside a simulation.

Traverse (thetraverse.co) is one example of a tool that is designed to help anyone explore and understand their own skills through AI-generated prompts and challenges. Traverse uses work simulation technology to assess learners' skills, then predicts future job success by analyzing those skills and matching students with suitable career paths. Based on the skill assessments, Traverse gives personalized insights and recommendations for career development. It also incorporates challenges that allow people to explore their potential in a practical and engaging way. These challenges can include real-world scenarios and tasks that simulate the demands of various careers. By participating in these challenges, learners can apply their knowledge and skills in a controlled environment to see how they perform. They'll also gain insights into areas where they excel and areas that may need improvement. Successfully completing challenges can boost learners' confidence in their abilities and may introduce them to career paths they weren't aware of before. Traverse also includes educational resources and courses that help people develop the skills needed for their chosen careers.

The potential impact of testing out careers before committing to a future pathway cannot be overstated. This approach helps learners make more informed decisions about their futures. By engaging in career simulations, they can experience firsthand what a particular job entails, allowing them to determine whether it aligns with their interests and strengths. This proactive exploration can save time and prevent costly changes in career paths later on by reducing the likelihood of students investing in education or training for careers that may not be the right fit for them.

The redefinition of career exploration transforms the traditional skills assessment or counseling center appointment. Instead of relying solely on static assessments and one-on-one counseling sessions, AI-driven simulations offer a dynamic and interactive way for learners to explore various career options. Simulations provide real-time feedback and allow for continuous learning and adaptation, which can make the career exploration process more engaging and effective. By integrating AI tools like Traverse, schools can offer a more personalized and immersive career counseling experience alongside human interactions and guidance.

VIDEO AVATARS

Imagine stepping into a classroom where historical figures come to life, literary characters leap off the pages, and fantastical creatures guide you through complex scientific concepts. This is the incredible power of video avatars, where educators, learners, and administrators can create dynamic, engaging, and personalized content that redefines the boundaries of traditional education. Video avatars, like those created with Immersive Fox, can represent the person creating them or be designed as characters from stories, historical figures, contemporary personalities, or even fantastical creations. This flexibility allows educators, learners, and administrators to explore new ways of presenting information and engaging with content.

Here are some of the possibilities:

- **Teachers:** Video avatars redefine the learning task by providing a versatile tool for creating interactive lessons and presentations. Teachers can embody historical figures to bring history lessons to life or create avatars that guide students through complex scientific concepts. This approach not only makes the content more engaging but also helps learners visualize and understand abstract ideas more concretely. Additionally, video avatars can be used to create personalized feedback and instructional videos, making learning more tailored and effective. In some learning management systems, educators can leave video feedback for their learners. Can you imagine opening the feedback for an assignment and being greeted by a cartoon avatar instead of your instructor?

- **Students:** Learners benefit from video avatars by being able to express their creativity and enhance their presentations. They might create avatars to represent characters in a book report, reenact historical events, or explain scientific phenomena. This makes their projects more interesting, especially for their peers to watch, and helps them develop digital literacy and storytelling skills. Furthermore, using avatars can reduce the anxiety some learners feel about public speaking, as they can present through their digital representations without being on-screen themselves.
- **Administrators:** Video avatars can create engaging communications and training materials. For instance, they can be used to deliver important announcements, conduct virtual tours of the school, or provide onboarding for new staff and students. This approach can make information more accessible and engaging, developing a more connected and informed school community.

VIDEO CREATION

Let's talk some more about video content. This is where generative AI begins to blow my mind, honestly. Creating videos as part of an educational task represents a significant shift from traditional assessments like essays or multiple-choice tests, obviously. But creating videos with AI is even more of a transformation.

Video creation requires us to engage in a multifaceted process that includes planning, scripting, filming, and editing. This process not only helps humans develop technical skills but also enhances our ability to communicate ideas effectively. Unlike traditional tasks, which often focus on isolated skills, video projects encourage us to synthesize information, think critically, and present a clear understanding of content in a creative and engaging manner. If someone has to understand a subject to write about it, they have to understand it even more deeply to make a video about it.

Video creation allows for a more personalized and authentic assessment of student learning. Each video project can reflect the unique perspectives and voices of the students, providing a richer and more nuanced understanding of their abilities and insights. This form of assessment also accommodates diverse learning styles, as students can express their knowledge through visual, auditory, and kinesthetic means. By incorporating elements such as storytelling, visual aids, and multimedia, students can create compelling narratives that demonstrate their mastery of the subject matter in ways that traditional assessments cannot possibly capture. Many educators have been using video creation tools with their learners for a long time. We get to level up video creation with AI support. It becomes less about learning how to make videos and more about the process holistically.

AI tools can assist in various stages of video production, from generating scripts and storyboards to editing and enhancing the final product. These tools can save time and reduce the technical barriers associated with video creation, making it more accessible to anyone who wants to be a creator. AI can provide personalized feedback and suggestions, helping humans improve their work and learn new skills. AI-generated videos can also be used to create interactive and adaptive learning experiences, where content is tailored to the individual needs and interests of each viewer.

Creating videos with AI tools offers several distinct advantages over traditional, manual video creation. One of the primary differences is the efficiency and speed that AI brings to the process. AI tools can automate many of the time-consuming tasks involved in video production, such as scripting, editing, and adding effects. For instance, AI can generate a script based on a simple prompt, select relevant images and video clips, and seamlessly edit them together. This automation allows creators to focus more on the creative aspects of their projects rather than the technical details.

Another significant difference is the level of accessibility that AI tools provide. Traditional video creation often requires specialized skills and software, which can be a barrier for many people. AI tools, however, are designed to be user-friendly and accessible to individuals with varying levels of expertise. This democratization of video production means that more people can create high-quality videos without needing extensive training or experience. While we still need people trained in film production in our world, it's exciting to think about how individuals without advanced training can still participate in creation opportunities.

AI tools also offer enhanced creativity and innovation. They can suggest new ideas, provide creative templates, and even generate unique visual and audio effects that might be difficult or time-consuming to create manually. For example, AI can analyze trends and audience preferences to recommend content that is more likely to engage viewers. This capability could allow creators to experiment with new styles and formats, pushing the boundaries of traditional video production. Overall, AI-assisted video creation makes the process faster, more accessible, and more innovative, enabling a wider range of people to produce professional-quality videos.

Tools for video creation are developing rapidly, and companies might mean different things when they say they're powered by AI. Some create videos straight from text prompts, while others are use AI to remove backgrounds or add sound effects. While all these features are helpful, some are arguably more impressive than others (although a good background remover is still priceless!). Canva for Education has been developing its AI-enhanced video features and will continue to advance that functionality. It's accessible and free for students of all ages, making it a great first step. WeVideo is another popular tool in education, and it has received some AI enhancements lately. It provides tools for green-screen effects, voice-overs, and motion titles, making it suitable for creating dynamic and engaging educational content.

Clipchamp is Microsoft's video creation tool for education (also free), and it has similar AI-powered design features.

Synthesia is an advanced AI video creation platform that allows users to generate high-quality videos using AI avatars and voice-overs. The platform is designed to be user-friendly, making it accessible to individuals with varying levels of technical expertise. With Synthesia, users can create videos by simply typing a script, selecting an AI avatar, and customizing the visuals. The AI then generates a realistic video in minutes, complete with natural-sounding narration and professional-quality visuals.

One of the standout features of Synthesia is its extensive library of AI avatars, which can speak in over 140 languages. This makes it an excellent tool for creating diverse and inclusive content. Users can choose from a variety of avatars to represent different characters, whether they are historical figures, contemporary personalities, or fictional creations. This flexibility allows educators to bring lessons to life in a way that is engaging and relatable for students.

Synthesia also offers a range of customization options, including the ability to edit scripts, change backgrounds, add music, and animate on-screen elements. These features make it easy to create dynamic and interactive videos that capture the viewer's attention. Additionally, Synthesia's collaboration tools allow users to share their videos with others for feedback and further refinement, making it a powerful tool for group projects and collaborative learning. Synthesia redefines video creation by making it faster, more accessible, and more innovative. It enables educators, students, and administrators to produce professional-quality videos that enhance learning and communication.

If you're looking for a low-level video creation entry point for animated shorts, try Plotagon. It's is an AI-powered animation tool that allows users to create stories by simply writing a script that the AI then generates characters, scenes, and animations for. It's particularly great for language arts and creative writing classes, but it could be used to create characters and scenes to describe any sort of content—including public service announcements for the school or community. Imagine learners creating an animated cartoon to teach others about an important issue. They focus on the script writing, and AI does the rest.

GAME CREATION

Game-based learning has been a focus of mine for at least the last ten years. I spent about five years working closely with "digital druid" Stephen Reid through our work at a nonprofit, Phygital Labs, and I tried to soak up as much genius as I could! Game-based learning is a powerful educational approach that leverages the engaging and interactive nature of games to enhance learning outcomes. It promotes active learning, critical-thinking, and problem-solving skills by immersing students in scenarios where they must apply knowledge and strategies to succeed. This method not only increases motivation and engagement but also promotes a deeper understanding of the material. By integrating game mechanics into the learning process, educators can create a dynamic and stimulating environment that encourages students to take risks, experiment, and learn from their mistakes. There are several types of game-based learning, and that certainly isn't the focus of this book. But I feel I need to clarify that game creation for learners can include anything from gamifying content (like making a quiz for other students to take to earn points) to full game experiences (in which students build a game with characters and a narrative or some kind of challenge, like in Minecraft or Fortnite).

When learners transition from being consumers of content (looking at you, worksheets, textbooks, PDFs, and videos) to creators of content, the educational experience shifts from traditional to transformational. In traditional learning, students passively receive information, often leading to surface-level understanding. However, as creators, students engage in higher-order thinking and creativity, designing and developing their own games. This process requires them to synthesize knowledge, apply interdisciplinary skills, and collaborate with peers.

It also gives people an outlet to a different world, separate from their own. In *Reality Is Broken*, Jane McGonigal argues that video games fulfill genuine human needs and have the potential to solve real-world problems by leveraging the motivational and collaborative power of game design. There's a myriad of AI platforms to support learners in creating rich, interactive content. This shift not only enhances their technical skills but also promotes a sense of ownership and agency in their learning journey.

I'm not an expert gamer. It takes a little extra effort for me to come up with game ideas, like I imagine some people get stuck writing or solving math problems. That means for me, AI support is incredibly helpful to get me started. Even without an idea to begin with or a knowledge of coding or design, learners can build a product with some support. AI game creation tools like Rosebud AI and Ludo.ai can significantly enhance this process by making game creation more accessible and efficient.

Rosebud AI is an AI-powered game development platform that allows users to create games by simply describing their ideas. The AI then generates the initial code. This makes game development accessible even to those with limited coding experience. The platform offers tools for creating game assets, character animations, and AI-driven NPCs (nonplayer characters) that react intelligently to players. Rosebud AI is made for education. It provides explanations of the generated code and allows for the creation of AI characters that can act as teaching assistants.

Ludo.ai is designed to streamline the game development process. It offers several features that make it ideal for educational settings, helping users generate new game concepts, elements, and mechanics by entering key words or phrases. This can spark new ideas and assist in overcoming creative blocks. The platform provides real-time market insights and trends, helping users make data-driven decisions about their game designs. Ludo.ai includes tools for generating game visuals, icons, and artwork, making it a one-stop solution for game development.

For mini games, try using Canva Code. It's simple, straightforward, and allows people with no coding experience at all to create small games that can be published for others to use. I imagine students building games for each other and then participating in a gallery walk to play each other's activities.

Taskade is another particularly useful platform that offers an AI educational game generator. It allows game developers (a.k.a. you or your learners!) to create dynamic and interactive educational games that make learning more engaging. And don't forget to check out Scenario for designing game art too.

AI game creation tools can redefine learning tasks in several ways:

- **Enhanced creativity:** Students can explore their creativity by designing unique game worlds and characters.
- **Interactive learning:** Games can make learning more interactive and engaging, helping students retain information better.
- **Real-world skills:** Developing games helps students acquire valuable skills such as coding, problem-solving, and project management.
- **Personalized learning:** AI tools can tailor the learning experience to individual students' needs and interests, making education more personalized and effective.

SONG CREATION

Just like game creation, song creation offers a dynamic way for students to express their understanding and creativity. Both processes involve storytelling, design, and technical skills, making them powerful tools for learning. AI tools can simplify and enhance these creative processes, providing new ways for students to showcase their learning. AI-generated music works by analyzing vast amounts of musical data to identify patterns and structures, which it then uses to create new compositions. Tools like Amper, AIVA, and SOUNDRAW allow users to generate music by selecting parameters such as mood, genre, and instrumentation.

AI-generated music can support learning in several ways. First, it can be used to create engaging and memorable introductions to new topics, helping to capture students' interest and set the tone for the lesson. Second, AI-generated music can enhance storytelling and multimedia projects by providing custom soundtracks that make presentations more immersive and captivating. Third, it can be used to create personalized learning experiences, such as custom songs for brain breaks or movement activities, which can help refresh and refocus students' minds. By integrating AI-generated music into the classroom, educators can create a more engaging and personalized learning environment that supports students' creativity and learning. There are two big apps for music generation that you might check out: Suno and Udio.

Using Suno to create AI-generated music is straightforward and user-friendly. Here's a brief overview of how to get started:

1. Start by visiting the Suno website and creating an account. You can log in using Google, Microsoft, or Discord.
2. Once logged in, click on the Create button. You can choose between Simple Mode and Custom Mode. In Simple Mode, you enter a brief description of the song you want to create, including details like genre, mood, and instruments.
3. After you enter your description, Suno will generate a song based on your input. You can choose to include vocals or keep it instrumental.
4. Listen to the generated song and make any necessary adjustments. In Custom Mode, you have more control over specific elements of the song.
5. Once you're satisfied with the song, download it and share it as needed—add it to a video or game as a soundtrack, or make it the entire project!

Suno makes it easy for anyone to create unique and personalized music, even without extensive musical knowledge. This tool can be particularly useful in educational settings, where students can use it to enhance their projects and presentations with custom soundtracks. AI-generated music offers possibilities for educators to redefine a task from traditional to creative, stretching learner imagination.

ILLUSTRATIONS

AI-generated illustrations offer a way to redefine what it means to create art—and the purpose behind it. Often in education, we see art as a supplement for other work products. Art supports writing or even game design. Unless it's specifically an art class, learners are often making art as an integration to other curricula.

Anyone can use AI tools to create art that goes beyond traditional methods, enabling them to produce detailed and imaginative visuals that bring their stories to life. Through advanced algorithms and vast data sets, AI tools generate art that not only reflects the narrative but also captures the emotional tone of a story. This technology allows students to craft illustrations with a level of complexity and creativity that might be difficult to achieve on their own, offering new possibilities for artistic expression. I already wrote about using AI to generate images, but I'm discussing it again here so we can dive deeper.

When art is the focus, we are redefining the activity. The work product becomes art itself.

AI art-generation tools such as ChatGPT, Gemini, Midjourney, Ideogram, Microsoft's Designer, Canva, and Suno use machine learning models trained on extensive data sets of images and styles. These tools can interpret textual descriptions and generate corresponding visuals, aligning closely with a user's vision. The process is straightforward: Users input a description of what they want, the AI generates multiple images, and then users can refine the final selection to better match their desired outcome. The iterative work involved with refining digital art can take as much critical thinking as other tasks, including making traditional art.

There's also a tool called Scribble Diffusion that helps turn hand drawings and rough sketches into more refined images. This is particularly helpful to people who have a vision for a work but prefer to have support in creating it. This app bridges the gap between imagination and visual representation. Begin by creating a sketch. Then upload to Scribble Diffusion. AI processes the sketch, then adds details and elements to create an image. Review the generated image and adjust as needed.

AI illustrations can serve as a central learning tool in various contexts. In language arts and creative writing, students can use AI tools to create vivid illustrations that accompany their narratives, allowing the visual aspect to be the primary work product. Instead of simply supplementing text, the illustrations become the storytelling medium, with students crafting detailed depictions of characters, settings, and moods that immerse the audience in their story.

SCAVENGER HUNTS AND ESCAPE ROOMS

Scavenger hunts and escape (or breakout) rooms have been used in education for a long time. It takes a bit of work for teachers to create these lessons, including clues and sometimes hands-on manipulatives like locks and hidden elements. Activities like these combine the thrill of exploration—and often competition—with learning. With AI generating content and spaces for these activities, teachers can redefine the learning environment without doing all the work themselves.

AI-powered scavenger hunts and escape rooms typically involve using AI tools to create and manage the hunt. For example, educators create—or use AI to generate—a series of clues or tasks that students need to complete. These can be related to the curriculum, such as finding historical facts, solving math problems, or identifying scientific concepts. AI tools can also be used to provide hints or verify answers. Learners might use an AI chatbot to ask for hints or confirm if they've found the correct answer. Educators could even set up a chatbot that helps guide students without giving away an answer. A scavenger hunt can be hosted on digital platforms (Genially and ThingLink come to mind) that support interactive elements such as QR codes, multimedia content, and real-time feedback.

AI can help tailor the difficulty level of clues based on students' individual abilities. By analyzing past performance or progress, AI tools can adjust tasks to ensure that they are appropriately challenging for each learner. AI-powered escape rooms can integrate multiple subjects into a single experience. For example, students might need to solve a math problem to unlock a historical fact, combining math, history, and critical-thinking skills in one task. AI can help weave these subjects together, creating a more holistic learning environment. Sometimes these clues are more difficult to think of, and using AI to generate them is a big help.

These activities can simulate real-world problem-solving scenarios, such as environmental issues or technological problems, where students must apply what they've learned to "escape" or complete a hunt. This situational learning adds relevance and context to the curriculum. AI can also introduce elements of gamification, such as tracking progress, awarding points or badges, and providing instant feedback to increase student motivation. Adaptive AI can make the activity more competitive or collaborative.

Room2Educ8 has an entire framework and published paper on how to create digital escape rooms using generative AI!

Goosechase is a common app that people all over the world use to create mission-style, highly interactive scavenger hunts. It's free to start, and it's also great for adult staff retreats or gamified gatherings. In September 2024, Goosechase got funding to develop an AI agent that will help educators produce interactive content for their classrooms.

Hidden Door is a web-based application that allows people to play AI-generated games. But people can also create AI-powered games based on any content they like. It's a little bit choose-your-own-adventure meets video game, with an AI twist. I played through a version of *The Wizard of Oz* that was incredibly well designed. Anyone can create a scavenger hunt game through Hidden Door and publish it for others to play.

I used Canva Code to create an escape room too. It did a great job!

> **SAMPLE PROMPT**
>
> Create a virtual escape room for my fifth-grade students. They are learning about the solar system. Give them four riddles to solve, one at a time. Wait for them to answer each one. For each riddle, when they enter the correct answer, unlock one part of the interactive graphic. The graphic should be a door. Each part of the door is revealed as they respond appropriately to the puzzles.

Canva's AI generated the code for an activity that I could share in a Canva site or add to an existing design.

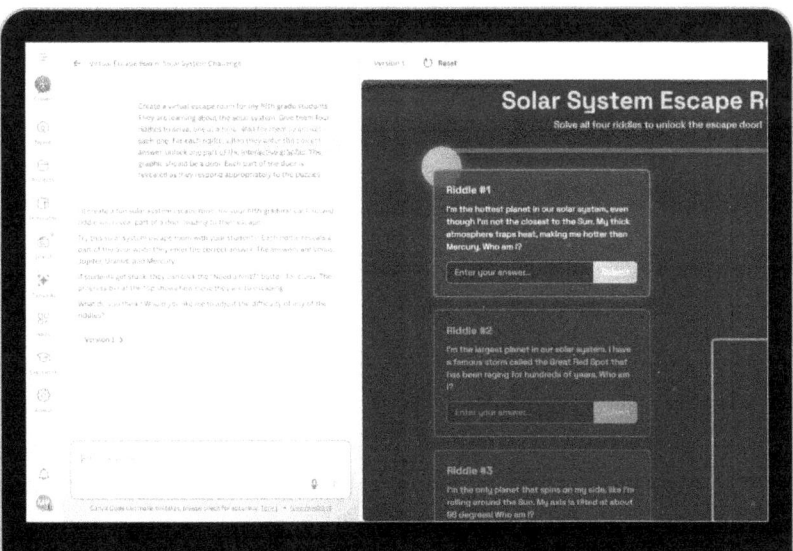

SIMULATIONS AND INTERACTIVES

Simulations and interactive web content represent a significant leap in educational technology. These tools go beyond the traditional by providing dynamic learning environments for anyone to explore, experiment with, and apply in real-world scenarios. Simulations and interactives fall into the redefine category because they enable learning experiences that were previously inconceivable without technology, and in many cases they completely change the task.

For example, instead of merely reading about historical events, students can participate in interactive simulations where they make decisions as historical figures, experiencing the consequences of their actions. This not only deepens their understanding but also makes learning more engaging and memorable. Similarly, interactive web content can provide real-time feedback and demonstrate how data points are connected, offering minds-on learning experiences that traditional methods cannot match. There are many ways to amplify critical thinking, computational thinking, and knowledge construction through minds-on learning.

Claude Artifacts and Canva designs are both powerful tools for creating interactive and immersive learning experiences. They allow anyone to generate substantial, stand-alone content that can be easily modified and built upon. I asked Claude to create a simulation of the tide chart in Seattle, Washington, for students to understand how the tide is associated with the phases of the moon. I also asked Canva AI to do the same thing. Both return shareable, interactive simulations, although I think Canva's design integration makes the results a bit more refined.

In this case, the task changes from reading a tide chart online and then finding the phases of the moon on a calendar to focusing on the correlation, using actual data and graphs. Educators can use results like these to generate interactives based on real-world data.

You can also use Claude or Canva AI to create simulations through code. Canva Code is especially helpful in education, since Canva is freely available for K–12 schools and has Anthropic's models built in. Canva adds its own design elements to the code, making visually lovely creations while staying safely inside the Canva platform. It's also super simple to publish the simulation to a Canva site. Keep in mind that students have access to this technology as well!

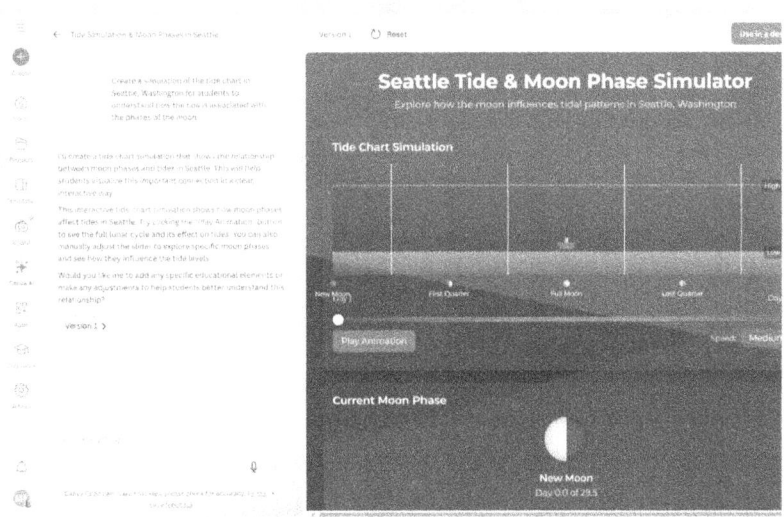

Simulation from Fable offers advanced AI-driven virtual environments where students can interact with AI characters and explore dynamic scenarios. For instance, in a business class, students could use Simulation to run a virtual start-up. They could make decisions about product development, marketing, and finances, then see the consequences of their choices in real time. This hands-on experience helps students understand complex business concepts and develop critical-thinking and decision-making skills.

Wharton Interactive provides a range of simulations designed to transform and democratize education. One example is the Saturn Parable, which teaches team leadership through a fast-paced, engaging scenario. Students work together to solve problems and make decisions, learning valuable leadership and collaboration skills in the process. Another example is the Entrepreneurship Game, where students experience running a high-growth start-up, learning about entrepreneurship, innovation, and strategic thinking.

AUDIO OVERVIEW

You already know about read-aloud and audiobooks, you've heard of AI-generated summaries, and at this point you even know about AI-generated audio and video. Combine these and you have audio overviews. I'm not sure, but I think the first tool to release this broadly was NotebookLM. Free with a Google account (and a completely different user agreement from Google Gemini, in which NotebookLM doesn't store your data or leave it open to human review), NotebookLM creates a podcast-style audio file based on the sources you add. There are immediate, powerful possibilities for this type of generative AI. Copilot Notebook also has this technology built in.

So, what makes this so impactful for education? Imagine you're trying to reach every student in your class. You've got kids who learn best by reading, others who prefer listening, and some who need both to really get it. Audio overviews hit that sweet spot. They're not just for students with reading difficulties or visual impairments, though they're a game-changer for those kids. They're for everyone who's ever thought, "I wish I could just listen to a quick rundown of this chapter." With the podcast-style format provided by tools like NotebookLM, people of all ages might be far more engaged than they would be by reading a text or summary.

Think about how this could work across different grade levels. With younger learners, have AI generate a fun audio summary of a storybook, getting kids excited about what they're about to read. Middle-level learners could use it to get the gist of their research sources without drowning in information. More mature learners could generate quick study guides for exams or get a handle on those tricky texts. And at the university level, imagine having an audio preview of your lecture before you even step into the classroom.

We're definitely talking about the redefinition level here. This isn't just doing old things in a new way; it's doing things we couldn't even dream of before. Want a personalized audio summary that adapts to each student's needs? Done. How about an interactive audio experience where students can ask questions and get answers on the fly? That's possible too. AI-generated audio overviews are shaking things up in education. They're making information more accessible, more engaging, and more adaptable to individual needs. We're not just talking about a cool new tech toy here. We're looking at a tool that could fundamentally change how we teach and learn. Be sure to double-check the audio overview files generated by AI before you distribute them—just like text and images and everything else, they might contain mistakes.

CONCLUSION

When it comes to redefining how we use artificial intelligence to impact teaching and learning, I have to share an amazing application of this technology. *Ada*, an innovative art installation located in building 99 on Microsoft's Redmond campus, is a remarkable fusion of architecture and artificial intelligence. Designed by Jenny Sabin as part of Microsoft's Artist in Residence program, *Ada* uses AI to analyze anonymized data from the building's occupants, such as facial expressions, voice tones, and language. This data is then translated into a dynamic display of color and light, creating a visual representation of the building's collective mood. The installation is constructed from 3-D-printed nodes, fiberglass rods, and fabric knit with photoluminescent yarn, allowing it to glow and change colors in response to the emotional data it processes.

The purpose of *Ada* extends beyond its aesthetic appeal; it serves as a research tool and an artistic expression that explores the intersection of technology and human experience. By visualizing emotional data through art and architecture, *Ada* encourages occupants to think about the role of AI in our lives and stimulates creative thinking across the organization. The installation embodies the potential of AI to enhance human interaction and understanding while also addressing concerns about the invasive nature of AI technologies. It aims to create a space that is both functional and expressive, celebrating AI as a tool for joyful creation and out-of-the-box thinking.

The installation is named after Ada Lovelace, the pioneering mathematician and first computer programmer. It honors her contributions to the field of computing and symbolizes the fusion of creativity and technical innovation. The installation's design and placement in building 99 reflect Microsoft's commitment to exploring the possibilities of AI in enhancing our built environment. While it's likely impossible to put an installation like this in your school building (nor should you, considering the data privacy problems), *Ada* serves as an inspiring example of how AI can be integrated into physical spaces to create interactive and responsive environments that encourage creativity, collaboration, and emotional awareness.

Redefining learning takes time, energy, creativity, and resources. I gave many examples in this chapter, and some of them can't be implemented immediately. For many educators, there will be new apps to research, websites to evaluate, and licenses to purchase. I realize none of that is simple. Some of these apps may even disappear soon (hopefully not before this book is published!). It is my hope that we can remember that while the tools might change, pedagogy does not. Learning environments that create previously impossible options for students can transform education in profound ways. By focusing on the principles of effective teaching and learning, and leveraging AI to enhance these practices, we can create dynamic, engaging, and personalized educational experiences that prepare students for their futures. Choose one or two of these strategies to begin, and find a tool that works for you. Then carry on!

12

CLOSING

THROUGHOUT THIS BOOK, WE'VE EXPLORED AI through the lens of what I call AI optimism—a view of AI's incredible potential to address long-standing educational challenges while acknowledging the very real concerns it raises. Designing more responsive learning experiences, creating more engaging content, providing personalized support, analyzing data more insightfully—we've seen how AI can enhance every aspect of education at each level of the SAMR framework.

What emerges from our journey isn't just a more efficient version of traditional education but an opportunity to reimagine what's possible when we use AI to amplify rather than replace human connection. The fundamental skills we explored in my other book, *Sail the 7 Cs with Microsoft Education*, remain essential focus points for education in an AI-enhanced world:

- **Critical thinking:** AI tools provide students with real-world data sets and simulations that require analysis, interpretation, and complex decision-making, enhancing their ability to think critically.

- **Community:** Simulations and interactive content teach students about global issues and civic responsibilities, developing deeper understanding of their role as global citizens.
- **Creativity:** AI-powered content-generation tools allow students to express themselves in new formats, bringing their ideas to life and exploring different creative mediums.
- **Collaboration:** AI facilitates teamwork by providing platforms where students can work together regardless of location, with personalized support tailored to each student's needs.
- **Communication:** AI assistants help students practice and improve their communication skills through instant feedback and meaningful conversations.
- **Computational thinking:** AI tools involving coding, algorithm design, and data analysis enhance students' ability to approach problems methodically using logical reasoning.
- **Changemaking:** AI-driven curiosity coaching and personalized learning experiences help students develop resilience, empathy, and a growth mindset.

As we implement AI in education, several important considerations deserve our attention. The potential for bias in AI algorithms requires vigilance to ensure these tools promote fairness and inclusivity. As Ken Shelton and Dee Lanier remind us in their book, *The Promises and Perils of AI in Education*, "Embracing this moment as an inflection point allows us to chart a new course towards justice and empowerment."[3]

While AI can significantly enhance educational experiences, it cannot replace the unique qualities that human teachers bring to the classroom. Empathy, intuition, and meaningful relationships are irreplaceable human elements crucial for developing a supportive and engaging learning environment. Educators should view AI as a tool to

---

3   Ken Shelton and Dee Lanier, *The Promises and Perils of AI in Education: Ethics and Equity Have Entered The Chat* (Lanier Learning, 2024).

augment their teaching, not as a substitute for the invaluable human connection that defines effective education.

We must also teach students to critically evaluate AI outputs rather than trust them implicitly, promoting critical-thinking skills while avoiding the risk of anthropomorphizing these systems. Equally important is addressing data privacy concerns through transparent policies about how information is collected, used, and stored. The digital divide presents another challenge, as not all students have equal access to necessary technology—a disparity we must address to ensure AI becomes a tool for leveling the playing field instead of widening existing gaps.

The impact of AI in education, framed within the SAMR model, offers exciting possibilities at every level. From simple substitution of traditional tools with digital alternatives to the redefinition of learning through immersive environments and personalized support, AI can help us reimagine education in ways that deepen student learning and empower educators to transform their practice.

Your role as an educator has never been more important. The most powerful educational technology is only as impactful as the human wisdom guiding its implementation. Your creativity, ethical judgment, and understanding of your learners' needs will determine whether AI becomes just another digital tool or truly transforms education.

When I watch my own children and other students in schools interact with AI today, I get a glimpse of the extraordinary possibilities that lie ahead. They are not just consuming content but collaborating with it to create, explore, and solve problems. Their understanding of AI as a natural thinking partner gives me hope that the next generation will achieve much more than we can imagine.

I invite you to begin your journey with small, meaningful steps. Choose one area where AI might enhance your practice, experiment thoughtfully, learn from both successes and setbacks, and gradually expand your vision. Share your discoveries with colleagues, advocate for thoughtful implementation in your institution, and remember that you are helping to shape not just how AI is used in education today but how it will evolve tomorrow.

The future of education won't be created by algorithms or magic. It will be led by educators who approach technology with both optimism and wisdom. With AI as our partner rather than our replacement, we can create learning experiences that are more engaging, more equitable, and more deeply aligned with the timeless human purpose of education: helping each learner discover and develop their unique potential.

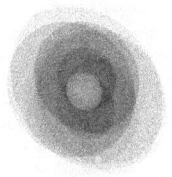

APPENDIX

THESE SELF-ASSESSMENTS ARE DESIGNED TO help you evaluate how you currently use generative AI in your teaching and how you might deepen its impact on student learning. Based on the SAMR (substitution, augmentation, modification, redefinition) model, the assessments will guide you through four levels of technology integration, from basic substitution to uses that redefine what's possible in education.

Each level of the SAMR model provides examples and prompts to help you assess your practice and reflect on ways AI can improve efficiency, foster creativity, or enhance student engagement. Whether you're just beginning your journey with AI or looking for ways to push your use of technology to the next level, this tool is designed to meet you where you are.

This self-assessment will help you to do the following:

- Understand how generative AI is currently impacting your teaching and student outcomes.
- Identify areas where you could expand or modify your use of AI to enhance learning.
- Explore innovative ways to use AI that encourage creativity, critical thinking, and problem-solving in your students.
- Use this tool as an opportunity to reflect, plan, and envision how AI can become a meaningful part of your classroom or school, ultimately helping your learners engage in deeper, more authentic learning experiences.

TEACHER SELF-ASSESSMENT

1. Substitution: Technology as a Direct Tool Substitute

Are you using generative AI tools to replace a traditional task without changing the task?

> **EXAMPLE 1:** You use AI to generate essay prompts instead of creating them manually.
>
> **EXAMPLE 2:** You use AI to generate worksheets, lesson plans, or quizzes instead of creating them by hand.
>
> **EXAMPLE 3:** You use AI to write summaries or explain concepts.

Is there any significant functional change in how students complete the task, or is it just a faster way to accomplish the same outcome?

> **EXAMPLE:** You use AI to write short summaries or explanations but without deeper engagement or altered expectations.

SELF-ASSESSMENT:

- ☐ I use AI to generate simple resources like worksheets, quizzes, or lesson plans that would traditionally be made manually.
- ☐ AI speeds up the creation of teaching materials. The learning outcomes and engagement remain unchanged.
- ☐ I employ AI to automate aspects of lesson planning or content delivery without altering the structure of the task.

2. Augmentation: Technology as a Direct Tool Substitute, with Functional Improvement

Is AI improving the efficiency or quality of the task?

> **EXAMPLE 1:** AI tools help students identify and correct grammatical mistakes in their writing.
>
> **EXAMPLE 2:** AI-powered tools give personalized feedback on assignments, providing suggestions for improvement.
>
> **EXAMPLE 3:** AI creates more adaptive or differentiated quizzes based on individual student performance.

Does the AI offer improvements that traditional methods cannot provide, such as immediate feedback, grammar checks, or adaptive learning suggestions?

SELF-ASSESSMENT:

- [ ] I use AI to offer personalized, real-time feedback that enhances students' learning experience.
- [ ] AI tools improve the quality of student work, such as through enhanced grammar and structure in writing tasks.
- [ ] I use AI to adapt assignments, quizzes, or activities in real time, based on individual student performance.

3. Modification: Technology Allows for Significant Task Redesign

Are students engaging in tasks that have been significantly redesigned due to AI?

> **EXAMPLE 1:** Students interact with AI-powered chatbots to simulate real-world conversations, such as with historical figures, customer service reps, or peers.

EXAMPLE 2: Students collaborate with AI to co-create multimedia presentations, stories, or digital artwork.

EXAMPLE 3: Students use AI-driven voice recognition tools to practice communication skills, receiving instant feedback.

Is AI influencing the way students think or approach the task, leading to a more interactive or creative learning process?

SELF-ASSESSMENT:

- ☐ AI allows for more complex or creative student projects, such as multimedia or interactive work that involves substantial input from the technology.
- ☐ The tasks students complete are significantly different from traditional tasks because AI enables deeper engagement, creative expression, or critical thinking.
- ☐ Students use AI to analyze data or information in ways they couldn't do manually, changing their approach to research and learning.

4. Redefinition: Technology Allows for the Creation of New Tasks Previously Inconceivable

Are students using AI to engage in tasks that were not possible before the integration of this technology?

EXAMPLE 1: Students design their own AI chatbots or virtual assistants to solve specific problems or provide information for peers.

EXAMPLE 2: Students use AI to create and refine digital art, music, or immersive experiences like virtual reality tours.

EXAMPLE 3: AI is used to create interactive simulations or scenarios that allow students to explore real-world applications (e.g., historical reenactments, scientific experiments).

EXAMPLE 4: AI helps students analyze large data sets or simulate complex real-world systems, like climate models or economic forecasting.

Does AI enable students to explore new forms of expression, analysis, or creation that redefine the learning experience?

EXAMPLE: Students develop AI-powered tools that can address real-world issues like accessibility for people with disabilities or language translation for cultural exchange.

SELF-ASSESSMENT:

- ☐ Students are involved in creating AI-powered solutions, simulations, or digital experiences that redefine traditional learning outcomes.
- ☐ AI allows students to conduct complex analyses or engage in creative work that was not possible in traditional classroom settings.
- ☐ AI integration has transformed the classroom into a space where students are creators and innovators, not just passive learners.

Reflection:

- Where do I fall in the SAMR model right now?
- What opportunities do I have to shift from substitution or augmentation to modification or redefinition?
- How can I leverage generative AI to offer my students new opportunities for creativity, exploration, and deeper engagement with content?
- Am I ensuring that AI integration enhances critical thinking, collaboration, or problem-solving in ways that would be challenging without the technology?

ADMINISTRATOR SELF-ASSESSMENT

1. Substitution: Technology as a Direct Tool Substitute

Are you encouraging the use of generative AI tools to replace traditional tasks without changing the task?

Example 1: You promote the use of AI to generate administrative reports instead of creating them manually.

Example 2: You use AI to automate routine communications, such as newsletters or announcements.

Example 3: You implement AI for scheduling and resource management tasks.

SELF-ASSESSMENT:

- [ ] I model the use of AI to streamline administrative tasks such as generating reports or managing schedules.
- [ ] AI tools are used to speed up routine tasks without changing the fundamental nature of these tasks.
- [ ] I encourage staff to use AI for efficiency in administrative processes, maintaining the same outcomes.

2. Augmentation: Technology as a Direct Tool Substitute, with Functional Improvement

Is AI improving the efficiency or quality of administrative tasks?

EXAMPLE 1: AI tools help analyze student performance data to identify trends and areas for improvement.

EXAMPLE 2: AI-powered tools provide personalized feedback on teacher evaluations, offering suggestions for professional development.

EXAMPLE 3: You use AI to enhance communication with parents and the community through personalized messages and updates.

SELF-ASSESSMENT:

- [ ] I use AI to provide real-time, data-driven insights that enhance decision-making processes.
- [ ] AI tools improve the quality of administrative tasks, such as through detailed data analysis and personalized feedback.
- [ ] I encourage the use of AI to adapt administrative processes in real time based on data and feedback.

3. Modification: Technology Allows for Significant Task Redesign

Are administrative tasks being significantly redesigned due to AI?

EXAMPLE 1: You implement AI-driven platforms for professional development, offering personalized learning paths for teachers.

EXAMPLE 2: You use AI to facilitate virtual meetings and collaborative planning sessions with staff.

EXAMPLE 3: You use AI tools for predictive analytics to forecast enrollment trends and resource needs.

SELF-ASSESSMENT:

- [ ] AI allows for more complex and efficient administrative processes, such as personalized professional development plans.
- [ ] The tasks I oversee are significantly different from traditional tasks because AI enables deeper data analysis and strategic planning.
- [ ] I use AI to redesign administrative workflows, leading to more effective and informed decision-making.

4. Redefinition: Technology Allows for the Creation of New Tasks Previously Inconceivable

Are you using AI to engage in tasks that were not possible before the integration of this technology?

> **EXAMPLE 1**: You develop AI-powered systems for real-time monitoring of school safety and security.
>
> **EXAMPLE 2**: You use AI to create immersive virtual tours of the school for prospective students and parents.
>
> **EXAMPLE 3**: You implement AI-driven platforms for community engagement and feedback collection.
>
> **EXAMPLE 4**: You use AI tools for advanced predictive modeling to inform long-term strategic planning.

SELF-ASSESSMENT:

- [ ] I lead initiatives that involve creating AI-powered solutions for school safety, community engagement, and strategic planning.
- [ ] AI allows for innovative administrative practices that were not possible in traditional settings.
- [ ] AI integration has transformed the administrative landscape, enabling new forms of engagement, analysis, and strategic planning.

Reflection:

- Where do I fall in the SAMR model right now?
- What opportunities do I have to shift from substitution or augmentation to modification or redefinition?
- How can I leverage generative AI to offer new opportunities for efficiency, strategic planning, and community engagement?
- Am I ensuring that AI integration enhances decision-making, collaboration, and problem-solving in ways that would be challenging without the technology?

BOOK STUDY INFORMATION

Looking to lead a book study with this book? Check out resources, place a bulk order, and even request an author talk at beckykeene.com/books.

ACKNOWLEDGMENTS

THE CONTENTS OF THIS BOOK were shaped by educators around the world who have pushed me to think differently and are willing to have critical conversations about both the benefits and challenges of artificial intelligence in our schools. I'm grateful to all of you who guide others while keeping education meaningful and relevant—especially the ones who let me borrow your classrooms and work with your students.

My sincere thanks to each of the women in AI who previewed and endorsed this work. Your support demonstrates the collaborative approach that makes our field stronger.

This book wouldn't exist without Dave, Tara, and Sal at DBC, Inc. Books. You believed in my ideas and provided the perfect balance of guidance and freedom to develop them.

I'm fortunate to work with Dr. Kim West and the entire team at i2e. Kim, your leadership has given me opportunities to connect with educators globally, experiences that have deepened my understanding of AI's role in diverse learning environments. I am so grateful.

A special note of gratitude to Mark Sparvell for introducing me to Dr. Ruben Puentedura and to Dr. Puentedura for jumping in so enthusiastically when I asked him to contribute.

These pages reflect not just my own work but insights from a community committed to educational transformation—thank you all for contributing to this journey.

Finally, thank you to my children for always being my test agents and keeping me grounded in the realities of education. Bouncing ideas off you, learning from you, and listening to you is a joy. Keep thinking critically and asking big questions. I'm proud of you both.

ABOUT BECKY KEENE

AFTER SPENDING FIFTEEN YEARS AS a classroom teacher and instructional technology program specialist in Kent School District, Becky Keene now works as director of operations for insight2execution. She oversees the team of managers and professional learning specialists in developing content for edtech companies worldwide as well as delivering training engagements and implementation planning for systemic change with major education systems around the United States. Becky is the coauthor of the Microsoft Certified Coach program, which focuses on instructional coaching best practices.

Becky chose to focus on generative AI in education as an opportunity to implement twenty-first-century learning strategies and empower students to be creators rather than consumers. She has shared her AI-optimistic viewpoint as a speaker at events such as Canva Create, BETT UK, regional AI summits, school district workshops, and ISTE Ignite, while also working with local schools and universities to develop AI adoption strategies and implementation plans.

Becky is the coauthor of *Sail the 7 Cs with Microsoft Education*. She holds an MSEd degree in early literacy, is a National Board Certified Teacher in ELA for early adolescence, and is an ISTE Certified Educator. She is also a LinkedIn Learning instructor with several courses on a variety of topics, including AI.

INVITE BECKY TO BRING AI OPTIMISM TO YOUR SCHOOL OR ORGANIZATION!

Becky Keene has traveled to work with teachers and school leaders around the world. She is an internationally recognized speaker and highly rated workshop facilitator.

Sample topics and workshops include:

- **AI Optimism:** Inspiring possibilities in an evolving reality
- **AI in Action:** Using generative tools to transform learning
- **From Idea to Impact:** Powerful prompt writing for generative AI
- **The 7 Cs and Beyond:** Strategies to engage and empower any learner
- **The Future of Education:** Bringing positive vision to a new reality

Becky's TikTalkWalks include thoughts and encouragement posted daily to social media. Follow Becky on TikTok, Instagram, or Threads to connect with her regular content.

Get in touch with Becky and subscribe to her newsletter and other updates at beckykeene.com.

MORE FROM  DAVE BURGESS Consulting, Inc.

Since 2012, DBCI has published books that inspire and equip educators to be their best. For more information on our titles or to purchase bulk orders for your school, district, or book study, visit DaveBurgessConsulting.com/DBCIbooks.

THE *LIKE A PIRATE*™ SERIES
Teach Like a PIRATE by Dave Burgess
eXPlore Like a PIRATE by Michael Matera
Learn Like a PIRATE by Paul Solarz
Plan Like a PIRATE by Dawn M. Harris
Play Like a PIRATE by Quinn Rollins
Run Like a PIRATE by Adam Welcome
Tech Like a PIRATE by Matt Miller

THE *LEAD LIKE A PIRATE*™ SERIES
Lead Like a PIRATE by Shelley Burgess and Beth Houf
Balance Like a PIRATE by Jessica Cabeen, Jessica Johnson, and Sarah Johnson
Lead beyond Your Title by Nili Bartley
Lead with Appreciation by Amber Teamann and Melinda Miller
Lead with Collaboration by Allyson Apsey and Jessica Gomez
Lead with Culture by Jay Billy
Lead with Instructional Rounds by Vicki Wilson
Lead with Literacy by Mandy Ellis
She Leads by Dr. Rachael George and Majalise W. Tolan

THE EDUPROTOCOL FIELD GUIDE SERIES
Deploying EduProtocols by Kim Voge, with Jon Corippo and Marlena Hebern

The EduProtocol Field Guide by Marlena Hebern and Jon Corippo

The EduProtocol Field Guide Book 2 by Marlena Hebern and Jon Corippo

The EduProtocol Field Guide Math Edition by Lisa Nowakowski and Jeremiah Ruesch

The EduProtocol Field Guide Primary Edition by Benjamin Cogswell and Jennifer Dean

The EduProtocol Field Guide Social Studies Edition by Dr. Scott M. Petri and Adam Moler

The EduProtocol Field Guide ELA Edition by Jacob Carr

LEADERSHIP & SCHOOL CULTURE

Be 1% Better by Ron Clark

Be THAT Teacher by Dwayne Reed

Beyond the Surface of Restorative Practices by Marisol Rerucha

Change the Narrative by Henry J. Turner and Kathy Lopes

Choosing to See by Pamela Seda and Kyndall Brown

Culturize by Jimmy Casas

Discipline Win by Andy Jacks

Educate Me! by Dr. Shree Walker with Micheal D. Ison

Escaping the School Leader's Dunk Tank by Rebecca Coda and Rick Jetter

Fight Song by Kim Bearden

From Teacher to Leader by Starr Sackstein

If the Dance Floor Is Empty, Change the Song by Joe Clark

The Innovator's Mindset by George Couros

It's OK to Say "They" by Christy Whittlesey

Kids Deserve It! by Todd Nesloney and Adam Welcome

Leading the Whole Teacher by Allyson Apsey

Let Them Speak by Rebecca Coda and Rick Jetter

The Limitless School by Abe Hege and Adam Dovico

Live Your Excellence by Jimmy Casas

Next-Level Teaching by Jonathan Alsheimer

The Pepper Effect by Sean Gaillard

Principaled by Kate Barker, Kourtney Ferrua, and Rachael George

The Principled Principal by Jeffrey Zoul and Anthony McConnell

Relentless by Hamish Brewer

The Secret Solution by Todd Whitaker, Sam Miller, and Ryan Donlan

Start. Right. Now. by Todd Whitaker, Jeffrey Zoul, and Jimmy Casas
Stop. Right. Now. by Jimmy Casas and Jeffrey Zoul
Teach Your Class Off by CJ Reynolds
Teachers Deserve It by Rae Hughart and Adam Welcome
They Call Me "Mr. De" by Frank DeAngelis
Thrive through the Five by Jill M. Siler
Unmapped Potential by Julie Hasson and Missy Lennard
When Kids Lead by Todd Nesloney and Adam Dovico
Word Shift by Joy Kirr
Your School Rocks by Ryan McLane and Eric Lowe

TECHNOLOGY & TOOLS

50 Things to Go Further with Google Classroom by Alice Keeler and Libbi Miller
50 Things You Can Do with Google Classroom by Alice Keeler and Libbi Miller
50 Ways to Engage Students with Google Apps by Alice Keeler and Heather Lyon
140 Twitter Tips for Educators by Brad Currie, Billy Krakower, and Scott Rocco
Block Breaker by Brian Aspinall
Building Blocks for Tiny Techies by Jamila "Mia" Leonard
Code Breaker by Brian Aspinall
The Complete EdTech Coach by Katherine Goyette and Adam Juarez
Control Alt Achieve by Eric Curts
The Esports Education Playbook by Chris Aviles, Steve Isaacs, Christine Lion-Bailey, and Jesse Lubinsky
Google Apps for Littles by Christine Pinto and Alice Keeler
Master the Media by Julie Smith
Raising Digital Leaders by Jennifer Casa-Todd
Reality Bytes by Christine Lion-Bailey, Jesse Lubinsky, and Micah Shippee, PhD
Sail the 7 Cs with Microsoft Education by Becky Keene and Kathi Kersznowski
Shake Up Learning by Kasey Bell
Social LEADia by Jennifer Casa-Todd
Stepping Up to Google Classroom by Alice Keeler and Kimberly Mattina

Teaching Math with Google Apps by Alice Keeler and Diana Herrington
Teaching with Google Jamboard by Alice Keeler and Kimberly Mattina
Teachingland by Amanda Fox and Mary Ellen Weeks

TEACHING METHODS & MATERIALS

All 4s and 5s by Andrew Sharos
Boredom Busters by Katie Powell
Building Strong Writers by Christina Schneider
The Classroom Chef by John Stevens and Matt Vaudrey
The Collaborative Classroom by Trevor Muir
Copyrighteous by Diana Gill
CREATE by Bethany J. Petty
Ditch That Homework by Matt Miller and Alice Keeler
Ditch That Textbook by Matt Miller
Don't Ditch That Tech by Matt Miller, Nate Ridgway, and Angelia Ridgway
EDrenaline Rush by John Meehan
Educated by Design by Michael Cohen, The Tech Rabbi
Empowered to Choose: A Practical Guide to Personalized Learning by Andrew Easton
Expedition Science by Becky Schnekser
Frustration Busters by Katie Powell
Fully Engaged by Michael Matera and John Meehan
Game On? Brain On! by Lindsay Portnoy, PhD
Guided Math AMPED by Reagan Tunstall
Happy & Resilient by Roni Habib
Innovating Play by Jessica LaBar-Twomy and Christine Pinto
Instant Relevance by Denis Sheeran
Instructional Coaching Connection by Nathan Lang-Raad
Keeping the Wonder by Jenna Copper, Ashley Bible, Abby Gross, and Staci Lamb
LAUNCH by John Spencer and A.J. Juliani
Learning in the Zone by Dr. Sonny Magana
Lights, Cameras, TEACH! by Kevin J. Butler
Make Learning MAGICAL by Tisha Richmond
Pass the Baton by Kathryn Finch and Theresa Hoover
Project-Based Learning Anywhere by Lori Elliott

Pure Genius by Don Wettrick
The Revolution by Darren Ellwein and Derek McCoy
The Science Box by Kim Adsit and Adam Peterson
Shift This! by Joy Kirr
Skyrocket Your Teacher Coaching by Michael Cary Sonbert
Spark Learning by Ramsey Musallam
Sparks in the Dark by Travis Crowder and Todd Nesloney
Table Talk Math by John Stevens
Teachables by Cheryl Abla and Lisa Maxfield
Unpack Your Impact by Naomi O'Brien and LaNesha Tabb
The Wild Card by Hope and Wade King
Writefully Empowered by Jacob Chastain
The Writing on the Classroom Wall by Steve Wyborney
You Are Poetry by Mike Johnston
You'll Never Guess What I'm Saying by Naomi O'Brien
You'll Never Guess What I'm Thinking About by Naomi O'Brien

INSPIRATION, PROFESSIONAL GROWTH & PERSONAL DEVELOPMENT
Be REAL by Tara Martin
Be the One for Kids by Ryan Sheehy
The Coach ADVenture by Amy Illingworth
Creatively Productive by Lisa Johnson
The Ed Branding Book by Dr. Renae Bryant and Lynette White
Educational Eye Exam by Alicia Ray
The EduNinja Mindset by Jennifer Burdis
Empower Our Girls by Lynmara Colón and Adam Welcome
Finding Lifelines by Andrew Grieve and Andrew Sharos
The Four O'Clock Faculty by Rich Czyz
How Much Water Do We Have? by Pete and Kris Nunweiler
P Is for Pirate by Dave and Shelley Burgess
A Passion for Kindness by Tamara Letter
The Path to Serendipity by Allyson Apsey
PheMOMenal Teacher by Annick Rauch
Recipes for Resilience by Robert A. Martinez
Rogue Leader by Rich Czyz
Sanctuaries by Dan Tricarico

Saving Sycamore by Molly B. Hudgens
The Secret Sauce by Rich Czyz
Shattering the Perfect Teacher Myth by Aaron Hogan
Stories from Webb by Todd Nesloney
Talk to Me by Kim Bearden
Teach Better by Chad Ostrowski, Tiffany Ott, Rae Hughart, and Jeff Gargas
Teach Me, Teacher by Jacob Chastain
Teach, Play, Learn! by Adam Peterson
Teaching Is a Tattoo by Mike Johnston
The Teachers of Oz by Herbie Raad and Nathan Lang-Raad
Teaching the Ms. Abbott Way by Joyce Stephens Abbott
TeamMakers by Laura Robb and Evan Robb
Through the Lens of Serendipity by Allyson Apsey
Write Here and Now by Dan Tricarico
The Zen Teacher by Dan Tricarico

CHILDREN'S BOOKS
The Adventures of Little Mickey by Mickey Smith Jr.
Alpert by LaNesha Tabb
Alpert & Friends by LaNesha Tabb
Beyond Us by Aaron Polansky
Cannonball In by Tara Martin
Dolphins in Trees by Aaron Polansky
Dragon Smart by Tisha and Tommy Richmond
I Can Achieve Anything by MoNique Waters
I Want to Be a Lot by Ashley Savage
The Magic of Wonder by Jenna Copper, Ashley Bible, Abby Gross, and Staci Lamb
Micah's Big Question by Naomi O'Brien
The Princes of Serendip by Allyson Apsey
Ride with Emilio by Richard Nares
A Teacher's Top Secret Confidential by LaNesha Tabb
A Teacher's Top Secret: Mission Accomplished by LaNesha Tabb
The Wild Card Kids by Hope and Wade King
Zom-Be a Design Thinker by Amanda Fox

www.ingramcontent.com/pod-product-compliance
Lightning Source LLC
Chambersburg PA
CBHW050519170426
43201CB00013B/2015